managing
your move

managing your move

The *Complete* Relocation Guide

Cathryn Duffy

TATE PUBLISHING & *Enterprises*

Published by Tate Publishing & Enterprises, LLC
127 E. Trade Center Terrace | Mustang, Oklahoma 73064 USA
1.888.361.9473 | www.tatepublishing.com

Tate Publishing is committed to excellence in the publishing industry. The company reflects the philosophy established by the founders, based on Psalms 68:11,
"The Lord gave the word and great was the company of those who published it."

Book design copyright © 2007 by Tate Publishing, LLC. All rights reserved.
Cover design by Chris Webb
Interior design by Jennifer Redden

Published in the United States of America

ISBN: 978-1-60247-453-6
07.05.02

I wish to dedicate this book to my dear mother, Ruth. Her love, wisdom and humor helped me through every transition I have faced. I continually feel her presence and draw strength from the beautiful memories she left behind.

Acknowledgements

I wish to thank my ambitious and loving husband for his demanding career which prompted our many moves and inspired me to write this book. I want to thank my precious daughters, Erin and Caitlin, for their encouragement with this project and for enduring the ramifications of so many relocations. In addition, I want to express my gratitude to Lois, Cyndi, Meg, Anne, Kathryn, Heather, Nancy O., Nancy S. and Christina for all their love and confidence building efforts. Caitlin and Meg were especially supportive with their many suggestions and frequent assistance throughout the entire writing process. Special thanks to Herb for his kind support and helpful advice; and to Janey for believing in my book and validating my idea. Finally, I want to thank Betsy, my life-long friend, who provided her knowledge, sensibility and shoulder whenever I have needed it.

Table of Contents

Foreword

As a child I moved every couple of years. My Dad, a rare breed today, spent forty three years working his way up through the ranks of NCR before retiring. Every time I turned around it seemed, the boxes would appear and the moving vans would pull up in front of the house. Note that I used the plural of the word van, because I come from a large family with six children and by the last few moves they could not fit our belongings into just one truck.

My five brothers and I are living proof that kids do survive the moves a family has to make. In fact, it is because we moved so much that our family is as close as we are. Every couple of years we would wake up in a new home in a new town. The one constant was that we had each other. Nothing can replace the security of a happy home and a loving family.

At that time I had no understanding of, or appreciation for the moving process itself. My parents made it all look so easy. I guess that's where the "through the eyes of a child" comes into play. In any case, I grew up a veteran of moving from place to place. As an adult I have continued the pattern. In fact, truth be told, I enjoy moving.

Those of you that are in the midst of a move probably think that

I am crazy, but there is a thrill in starting over. But resolutions to keep a neater house and have a more organized life are replaced by daily living, and soon we are who we are, in yet another location.

I have moved half way across the country and have moved two houses down the street. In fact, we lovingly kid our neighbors Don and Kelly that we liked them so much, we wanted to live on both sides of them! But, no matter how far, a move is just that—a move, with boxes to pack, trucks to load and details that require the utmost attention. Many times through the years I thought it would have been nice to have a handbook; a check list, *something*, *anything*, to simplify the process of moving!

Cathryn Duffy, the only person I know that has actually moved more times than I have, has put her experience to work and has created this step-by-step manual of the how-tos of moving. She carefully dissects the moving process into its working parts and offers anecdotes, facts and figures to get even the most inexperienced mover among us on the right path. She leaves no detail unaddressed.

If you are about to start the process of moving, relax and embrace the process. Let Cathryn's experience guide you through the intricacies of the move. Learn from her mistakes and those of the many that have moved before you. Try to stay on course, hard as that may be. We all wish, at one point, that we could click our ruby red slippers and be in that new place, that new life, because there truly is no place like home. But, until time travel and sleight of hand join forces, we have to put one foot in front of the other to get from place to place.

Remember that every new beginning comes from some other beginning's end. Look ahead. Begin planning, dreaming and hoping. Your new life is waiting around the corner, down the block or across the country!

Meg Barton
President
Marketing by Design

Preface

Book stores offer many different versions of wedding planners, estate planners and numerous "how to do" almost everything guides, but I do not recall seeing any comprehensive guides for one of life's most stressful undertakings–the move. I view this as a void that needs to be filled. It is my wish to provide a guide book that will be easy to understand, informative, helpful and possibly even humorous to the reader who is facing the daunting task of relocation. Although I am not a licensed realtor, mortgage broker, banker or an employee of a professional moving company, my vast experience as a frequent mover should qualify me as a relocation specialist. My husband's demanding career and professional aspirations required numerous address changes. I have lived in ten states across the United States (Illinois, Michigan, Ohio, Massachusetts, New Jersey, Pennsylvania, Florida, Connecticut, California, New York and Georgia) and have first hand knowledge of just about every possible moving scenario that might arise. I have learned from both my mistakes and successes. For simplification, I have arranged the chapters in chronological order and included checklists to assist you, the reader, as you proceed with your move. The helpful websites, companies and products I mention have not paid me to promote them. It is my hope that whether you are moving across country or just across town, you can feel as organized as possible and avoid some potential pitfalls by following the appropriate suggestions. I especially hope to help you enjoy your moving adventure as much as possible. If you are planning to relocate outside of the United States, you can follow some of my suggestions, but you will need further assistance from those who have moved beyond our borders. Good luck to all of you!

1 | The Big Decision

If you are holding this book in your hand, you are probably thinking about moving. You may be contemplating a short distance move or a long distance one. Your reasons to consider moving may be personal, professional or both. Regardless of your circumstances, a big decision is about to be made. A local move and a long distance move usually involve different decisions, but both require careful consideration and involve much organization for the process to go as smoothly as possible.

A local move is often a choice move involving a life-style change or the need for more appropriate housing. Parents with young children may need more space to accommodate an expanding family. Families with grown children or "empty nesters" may consider downsizing to simplify their lives or add to their discretionary funds. Singles and young couples may be looking to invest and build equity in real estate instead of paying to rent someone else's property.

A longer distance move may be prompted by a job transfer, career opportunity or the desire for a change of venue and a fresh start. Maybe your employer has an operation in another location and requests your presence there. Perhaps you have been offered a new job that requires you to move outside your current area. You might even dream of making your home in a more agreeable climate. Whatever your reasons for moving may be, I hope this book becomes a helpful reference tool.

Through my own moving experiences and from sharing stories with others, I have discovered that often all factors are not carefully and thoroughly evaluated prior to making such a large life altering decision. If an entire family is affected, each member's well-being needs to be considered. School age children should participate in family discussions leading up to the formation of a final decision. Being the "new kid" in school can be traumatic for any child, but if youngsters are involved in the process from the most initial point, they can gain from this experience. They can learn valuable life skills such as decision making, organizing, cooperating, transitioning, adapting and understanding the ramifications for the entire family. Whether the child truly has a say in the move or not, bringing youngsters into the discussions makes them feel a part of the process. For example, a new job in a different region might enhance the lifestyle of all members, but place great distance between relatives and friends. The family meetings might result in the cons outweighing the pros or vice versa. Perhaps the new area offers a more attractive climate that everyone will enjoy, but the school system may be inadequate and private school unaffordable. The desire for a larger home in the same area that will more comfortably accommodate a growing family may result in added costs and might put too much strain on the usual household budget. Each family has its own concerns. Be certain to discuss every possible benefit and consequence in great detail.

Developing a point system for evaluating positives and negatives could prove helpful at this point. A simple 1–10 scale might work. I suggest sharpening your pencil and making a thorough list of all the pros and cons and assign a point value to each one. Place the negative aspects in one column and the positives in the other. Add up the points on each side and see what you can conclude. Perhaps each family member should create an individual list ranking personal preferences and concerns prior to the group meeting. This exercise may encourage participation and recognition of each member's perspective. I urge you to take the time to carefully consider all opinions and options.

My own family made the mistake of moving for a promising career opportunity that we thought would be worth the sacrifices in order to meet some long term goals. In reality, what appeared to be a better opportunity did not work out as expected and the move created problems in both our personal and professional lives. A new job search ensued and another move shortly thereafter. This period was extremely difficult on our family. Whether the decision to move was the wrong one, or the job was the wrong job, the result was that we found ourselves somewhere we did not want to be.

In retrospect we would have probably made a different decision, but who knew what lay ahead? Periodically we still must work to overcome the obstacles that move threw in our path. We had already uprooted one teen and left another behind to finish her high school career. Moving the younger one again so soon was not a good option. Should some of us stay or all go? Our decision was to move the family in stages. Not the optimal decision for all of us, but the one that had to be made. We all suffered the consequences, but happily all have recovered and we have learned from our mistake. Never make a rapid decision that can have a large impact on your life.

When possible, a visit to the intended area is advisable. If this is impossible, gather as much information as you can through the library, websites and bookstores to help you learn about your potential new hometown. You may even know people who live or have lived in the proposed area who you can contact for firsthand information and advice. We spent a week in the San Francisco area prior to deciding to relocate there. We were so glad that we did, because we discovered that we liked much of what the area offered, but we also learned that the housing prices and cost of living were amongst the highest in the nation. The cost of housing was and is still high there. We discovered that a comparable home would cost about three times more than the value of the one we currently owned. It became imperative for my husband to negotiate more effectively with his future employer before agreeing to accept the job. Fortunately many employers in high cost areas are aware of this problem and may agree to alternative forms of compensation or be more willing to help those they are attempting to recruit. Discuss these concerns with your possible employer and you might work out a better arrangement than you had initially expected.

Most large towns and cities have their own websites that can be easily found through any major search engine such as www.google.com or www.yahoo.com. Before relocating to Florida, I found www.myflorida.com extremely worthwhile. Likewise, I found a wealth of information at www.Buffalo.com prior to moving to Buffalo, New York. Another important and informative website is www.realtor.com. Millions of home listings, features about most areas and even neighborhoods all over the country can be found on this sight. You can view the housing options available in varying price ranges in all fifty states. You will find listings of real estate agents in a particular area who can send you detailed information such as local school reports, maps, demographics, regional photographs, cultural highlights and current home listings. Don't hesitate to ask a realtor to send you every bit of information available about the area you are considering. Successful realtors view this as part of their job and are happy to do this in the hopes of gaining your valuable business.

Book stores and libraries often carry recent publications and information for just about any area of the United States. Access to a newspaper printed in the potential region can give you a fairly accurate "feel" for an area. Newspapers and travel guides for major cities and all U.S. states can be found online and at libraries and book stores. These guides offer regional descriptions, travel tips and maps as well as summaries, evaluations and suggestions for area attractions, restaurants and accommodations. Personally, I recommend Fodor's guides because I find their annually updated versions to be the most complete and easy to use.

Whatever search methods and resources you decide to utilize, be sure to take adequate time to thoroughly investigate and familiarize yourself with your possible future hometown before you make any final decision to move. When it comes to location, you know the qualities you and your loved ones value and what you don't. Together, create your own list of pluses and minuses and spend adequate time discussing and evaluating all possible consequences of relocation. Most importantly, for the sake of long term happiness, always avoid making a rash moving decision.

- List the positive and negative impacts this move might make on you and your family.

- Rank the importance of each possible impact on a scale of 1–10.

- Gather as much information as you can about your possible location.

- Visit the potential location if possible.

- Discuss the area you are considering with others who are familiar with it.

- Evaluate and discuss all your findings.

- Decide whether to move or remain at your current address.

2 | How to Get Started

If the result of your decision making process points to making the move, *do not panic!* Your mind can start to reel as you begin to think of all that needs to be accomplished to make the big transition a reality. I have always found that making a to-do-list for the next day prior to going to bed keeps my mind organized and my sanity intact. A large calendar with ample space for writing notes helps to keep your time organized and allows you to fill your days in an efficient manner. File folders will help you keep your notes and pertinent papers together and accessible. If you do not already have a large pad of blank paper for making lists, folders and a big calendar for time management, go out and buy them now. These tools will be especially important to you during potentially trying times. Put your priorities and schedule on paper, get it off your mind and then get a good night's rest every night. If you are computer proficient, you can set up your calendar and to-do-lists on the computer and print them out daily or weekly. Do whatever works best for you.

The first thing to think about is your current living situation. Are you living in a rental property or do you own your own home? If you are a renter, find those rental agreement papers and review all you agreed to when you signed the lease. How long are you required to reside there and pay the rent? What are the financial consequences if you terminate the lease prior to the lease expiration date? If there is a high demand for rental housing in your area, breaking a lease is easier and potentially much less costly than in an area where housing demands are low.

Perhaps you have the option of subletting the rental property until your lease period ends. Subletting enables another party to live in the residence and pay the monthly fees until your obligation ceases. Be sure to look into the legal ramifications before you sublet. You are not completely off the hook if something goes awry. The original lease is still yours and the ultimate responsibility is probably yours, regardless of who resides there, until the lease expires. Go to the landlord or landlady and get all the specifics and options for your particular situation. The good news for the renter is that you can walk away from the property after settling your lease obligations.

For those of you who own your home, you are going to have to go through the more complex process of selling a home. At the very least, you will probably have to find someone to lease or rent your property in order to pay your current mortgage so you can afford another home in a new area. Once again, seek legal advice and understand all the aspects of leasing if you consider this option. I highly recommend selling the property instead of leasing because of several horror stories I have heard from friends who chose the lease option. In these cases, their properties were in much poorer condition at the time the lease expired than when the tenants initially moved in. A battle over settling the cost of damages then ensued causing many negative feelings and sometimes ugly behavior.

If you become an absentee landlord because you live far away, you should hire a management company or at least someone to frequently "keep an eye" on the place and arrange for normal household maintenance such as yard care, structural care and trash pickup. If you do not keep tabs on the site, violations of the lease and disrespect of your property can occur. All my friends who have rented their property to another party for an extended period have said they would never lease their houses long term again unless it was to a very responsible and trustworthy friend or relative.

If you are really emotionally attached to your current home and/or think you may return to it someday, you may want to carefully consider leasing as an option. You may also want to retain the property for investment potential. Just be sure to hire an attorney to prepare legally binding lease documents to protect you and your house. If your finances allow you to maintain more than one house, the least you will need to do is hire a competent caretaker so your property will retain its value while you are living elsewhere.

Once you have thought about your now "temporary" place of residence, it is time to begin taking the necessary steps to move on and out of your current home.

Chapter Two Check List

- Obtain or set up a calendar, buy folders and make lists to manage your schedule.

- Consider your current living situation. Do you rent or own your home?

- Review your lease agreement and take appropriate action based on its specific terms.

- Decide whether to sell or lease your property if you own your home.

- Think of your present home as temporary housing.

3 | Preparing to Market Your Home

The vast majority of homeowners choose to sell their homes and then purchase another one in a new location. The selling process can be a time consuming, difficult and emotional experience. It is often the most significant part of the move for the seller. The steps of the moving process fall into place once the contract of sale is signed by both buyer and seller. If you follow my suggestions and remain optimistic, all will work out fine as soon as the "right buyer" comes along.

To begin with, try to view your home from the perspective of a potential buyer. Detach yourself from your emotions and view your home as merchandise that is for sale. Keep in mind that to you, your house is a home; to the buyer, it is real estate available for a price. Think about the overall condition of your property.

It is wise to have a complete professional home inspection done before you put forth any effort or expense into sprucing up the place. For example, it is futile to go ahead and paint the exterior if the siding requires some repair or replacement. A pest inspection is also a good idea. Termites and carpenter ants can cause severe damage that you will want to fix before marketing your home. If you own an older home built before 1978 be sure it is certified free of exposed lead paint or asbestos building materials. Both are considered to be environmentally hazardous. A radon evaluation is also an environmental concern in some locations around the country. If your home has a septic tank instead of a sewer system, you should pay for a water quality evaluation to alleviate the fears of those unfamiliar with this type of system. A potential buyer will more than likely require a complete home inspection as a contingency to their offer and cancel a contract of sale if any significant damage, deficiencies or hazards are discovered. By arranging for an inspection yourself prior to listing the property, you can potentially uncover problems that might cancel a contract. Fixing the problems will help alleviate future trouble. However, understand that anything of significance uncovered during an inspection, must be noted on a seller's disclosure form. I will discuss disclosure forms in chapter five.

Are there any repairs that you have procrastinated about completing? Have you neglected the yard work or household cleaning tasks? When did you last change the filters for the heater and air conditioner? When was the last time the carpet or the windows were cleaned? When were the interior and exterior painted? If you own pets, you must remove animal odors and stains from your entire property. You may love Spot or Kitty, but the potential buyer has no affection for your four legged friends and especially the scents and marks they leave behind. Often animal lovers become desensitized to their own pet's "fragrances"; so if you are unsure, ask a friend or realtor to honestly evaluate this issue for you. You can eliminate most pet smells by frequently bathing and grooming your animals. Also, clean or replace your pet's sleeping quarters. Have carpets, rugs and furnishings where pets frequent professionally cleaned especially for pet spots and odor removal. Supermarkets sell wonderful fabric deodorizers (I recommend Febreze) in the cleaning supply aisle that may also assist you with problem household odors.

Residual odors from smokers must also be eliminated. This cannot be emphasized enough! A professional service may be required to remove smoking odors and smokers must smoke outdoors at all times until the house is sold. The lingering odor from tobacco is a major deterrent to home sales. Your home must be at its absolute best before you place it on the market. Hire professionals to do the necessary work, or get busy! All buyers want a home in good condition. A home in pristine condition is even more desirable.

Realtors often use the term "curb appeal" to assess the overall attractiveness of a home's exterior. If your home has peeling paint, an unkempt lawn, overgrown landscaping or a driveway that needs repair, this is the time to evaluate the condition and spruce up everything. It is also best to remove yard ornamentation and children's toys from the exterior to avoid a cluttered look. You want your home to look picture perfect since numerous photos of your house will be used to advertise the listing of the property.

Depending on the season and climate, you must keep your lawn mowed, shrubbery trimmed and weeds pulled. Planting flowers also adds color and beauty to a home. If you are marketing your house during the winter months, you have to keep the driveway and walkways clear of snow and ice. Not only will your property look well maintained, but you alleviate the chance of having someone slip and fall, and then blame you for their own clumsiness. Avoid all possible liabilities.

It is equally important to objectively consider the décor you have chosen for your home. Perhaps you should solicit honest opinions from others and listen to their viewpoints. Walls painted with loud colors and dark carpets might suit your taste, but may not appeal to possible buyers. Neutral shades such as beiges and whites provide a clean, simple background that helps the buyer imagine his or her own belongings in the setting. You do not want to lose a prospective buyer because he/she is overwhelmed by hot pink walls and cannot see past them to even visualize living in the space. Buyers, for the most part, can only see what they see–not what can be. My own sister put a house up for sale and experienced little interest in her home until she changed the purple walls in one room, the rust colored walls in another room and the yellow and purple faux finish in her bathroom. Soon after making the alterations, broker-client activity picked up and the house was sold within a month. It is best to stick with neutral shades when selling your house. Think of it as turning your home into a blank artist's canvas that will enable the buyer to create his/her own desired look.

We all have a tendency to accumulate too much "stuff." If your closets, garage and basement are bulging and your living areas are cluttered, it is time to go through things and either throw away unnecessary items, donate them to a worthy charity or hold a garage/yard sale. It is crucial to have your home appear as spacious and clean as possible. Don't forget to clear your yard too. Faded lawn furniture, outdoor toys and tools should be neatly stored in an organized shed or garage, or put in the trash. Excess accessories and knickknacks should be removed from tables, and counters should be spotless and almost bare. Remember potential buyers are probably looking at new homes and existing homes if they are doing a thorough search. If a model home is your competition, make your home look as much like a model as possible. Anything you can do to create the illusion and appearance of spaciousness will translate into a better price.

Some of you are probably guilty of being "pack rats" and may require the assistance of a close friend or relative to talk you out of keeping the dress you wore twenty five years ago to your eighth grade graduation. Sorry, but people are no longer impressed with your high school letter jacket either, so get rid of it or put it in storage. These items have probably developed strange odors by this time anyway. Remember it is time to move on! You know who you are, so buy your friend lunch in exchange for his or her good advice and honest opinions.

The same advice applies to unnecessary furniture. Many people overcrowd rooms. Make sure all interior traffic patterns flow as openly and unobstructed as possible. If you feel you must hang on to excessive furnishings and accessories, put them in storage until your house is sold. The Yellow Pages list storage facilities in your locale. Examine several sites for cleanliness and security features and review the rental agreement prior to signing on the dotted line. Most places will allow you to rent the space on a month to month basis as needed. Make certain that you rent adequate space for your belongings, but do not pay for more than you really require. My husband and I rented storage space when we decided to market our home in Florida. Homes there have no basement, so our seasonal decorations and our daughter's college items were being stored in the garage. This gave the garage an undesirable cluttered look, so we moved these items to a storage facility while we were marketing the home. Please consider doing the same to help sell your residence.

If you have trouble completing the cleaning out process yourself, at the very least you should have a good friend or capable family member help you with this crucial step. Another option is to hire a professional organizer who will do the job as quickly and efficiently as possible from an impartial perspective. You can find a referral for this service by logging on to www.NAPO.com or by asking your real estate agent. NAPO is the acronym for National Association of Professional Organizers. This website should help you find someone to assist you near your home. Professional organizers can often help you with both the move out and move in details too.

Personally, I do not qualify as a "pack rat" because I have had to complete the weeding out task so much due to my family's frequent moves. Even with an organizer's personality I still have had ample things to get rid of as we moved from place to place. I had lots of things to dispose of when we were leaving Pennsylvania and heading to Florida. My children no longer needed their baby items and we would no longer have use for snow shovels or most of our heavy winter clothing. I decided to hold a garage sale and learned to never repeat the experience. You may want to try it and judge for yourself, but I found it time consuming and more work than it was worth. I advertised my sale in the local paper which cost about $20. I stated that the sale would begin at 8:00 A.M. on a Saturday morning, but instead, we had people coming to the door late Friday night and before dawn on Saturday to try to stake their claims before the sale began. People were grabbing things from each other and some even wanted to bargain over prices on items marked as low as ten cents. Some people find this entertaining, but I felt it was chaotic. My three days of work only netted $200! Perhaps you will have a better experience if you choose to sell your unwanted items yourself.

Ever since my garage sale fiasco, I have donated our usable, unwanted or unnecessary items to some of my favorite charities, and have been able to take advantage of tax credits while benefiting others in need. Surfing the web, gathering suggestions from friends and relatives and even looking through the newspaper and telephone book can help you find appropriate charities. Some of our daughters' toys went to the preschool where I taught. I delivered some of my clothing to a shelter for abused women. We donated an old computer to a school for children with special needs. My oldest daughter sent her gently used prom gowns and accessories to an organization that provides prom attire to girls who cannot afford to purchase new outfits for this important occasion. A resale shop that benefits cancer research received some of our furniture. The process of eliminating unnecessary belongings can turn into a really positive experience when you involve the whole family. Children can learn valuable lessons about giving to others and pitching in as part of a family when they help with this aspect of the move.

Whether you decide to hold a garage sale, rent a dumpster and/or donate, keep in mind, the more spacious, organized, clean and beautiful your home appears, the more it will attract a buyer willing to pay a higher price. Also, the more you get rid of, the less you will have to move, unpack and put away later! Think of it as making your life less complicated!

For those of you who feel severely overwhelmed at this point, you can relax. Help is available if you find this all too challenging. If you follow the advice discussed in the next chapter, you will hire a competent realtor and he or she can direct you to someone who can provide the appropriate assistance. Real estate agents usually know professionals who can "stage" your home to make it as desirable as possible. A very close friend of mine was recently faced with the difficult task of selling her parents' home when it was time for them to enter a nursing facility. The realtor suggested the family remove the belongings they desired and then a staging crew went to work organizing, cleaning, repairing and updating the interior décor. The result was fabulous! The house sold in a few short weeks for considerably more than it would have if the stagers had not been hired to enhance the property. The staging paid for itself many times over. This might be a viable option for your particular situation.

- View your home from the eyes of a prospective buyer.

- Hire an inspector to thoroughly evaluate your property.

- Hire a pest inspector to determine if pests are present and/or have damaged your home.

- Have your older home certified free of lead paint and/or asbestos building materials.

- Have a radon evaluation done if this is an environmental concern in your area.

- Have a water quality evaluation performed if you have a septic system.

- Complete ALL repairs and improvements pointed out by professional evaluations.

- Tidy up the yard. Prune hedges, weed beds, edge lawn, rake leaves, etc.

- Change heating and air conditioning filters.

- Paint or touch up exterior and interior as needed.

- Remove indoor smoke and pet odors with reliable deodorizers.

- Hire a professional cleaning service to eliminate carpet stains and stubborn odors.

- Enhance the exterior with flowers and plants if the weather permits.

- Neutralize your home's décor if you have used bold tones.

- Organize and clean every square inch of your home.

- Hire a professional organizer if you become too overwhelmed.

- Eliminate all clutter. This includes most knick knacks and even some furniture.

- Store those items you cannot part with in a short term rental storage space.

- Hold a garage/yard sale or donate usable goods to appropriate charities.

4 | How to Market Your Home

Now that you have your house looking its best, it is time to think about how to sell it. There are two approaches you can take. One, you try to sell it yourself and act as your own agent, or you can hire a licensed real estate agent to market it for you. The National Association of Realtors says only thirteen to eighteen percent of all homes sold between 1997 and 2001 were sold by the owners. Most people I know who attempted to sell their own homes became discouraged and eventually turned the selling process over to a professional realtor. I only recommend attempting to sell your home yourself if it is in an area with an extremely high housing demand or you already know of an interested buyer.

If you are in an area with few houses on the market and a growing population, it should be easier and quicker to sell. During the economic boom in the Silicon Valley area of California, houses were in such demand that homes often had multiple offers within days or weeks, with or without the assistance of a realtor. It seemed that all a homeowner had to do was put a sign in the yard, an advertisement in the newspaper and hold a weekend open house for the public to tour the home. That was not, and is still certainly not the case in most housing markets!

My husband and I sold our first home without a realtor. We were living in a "starter" style neighborhood of inexpensive homes in a desirable location of northern New Jersey. We had very little money for a down payment on another home and decided we would try to sell the house ourselves to save the realtor commission. We put an advertisement in the local newspaper and had several calls almost immediately. We asked the callers to bring qualification letters from a lender so we could be certain that they were capable of obtaining appropriate financing. We wanted to be sure we were dealing with serious house hunters before we opened our door to strangers. We had a contract of sale in just six days! Remember, this is highly unusual and even though we had such a positive experience with our first sale, we never attempted to try to sell property on our own again. Job changes prompted all our subsequent moves so we were eager to relocate as quickly as possible. We felt we needed the expertise of a professional realtor who could provide knowledgeable advice, more property exposure and security. Carefully evaluate your situation before deciding what direction you will take to market your home.

You may want to consider selling your home without the aid of a licensed real estate broker if you already know of an interested party. I am aware of one couple who had a friend who admired their house so much that they offered to buy it if they ever wanted to sell. Their friends did indeed purchase the house a couple years later. My in-laws had the rare experience of having someone simply knock on their door to ask if they were interested in selling their home. The woman made an attractive offer and the papers were signed several days later. These situations are not commonplace, but maybe you will be just as fortunate. It certainly doesn't hurt to mention your intentions to sell to everyone you know in the event that they may already be interested in your property. If you do have a serious buyer, all you will really need to do is obtain the services of an attorney who specializes in real estate transactions. The attorney will provide you with all the necessary documents to write a sales contract and then assist with the sale or closing of your property. He or she is qualified to take you step by step through the process that can vary greatly from state to state. I urge you to hire a licensed real estate attorney if you are selling without using the services of a realtor. He or she will guide you, protect you and make the entire transaction legitimate. Seek referrals from friends to help you select an appropriate lawyer.

When I first began my moving adventures over twenty four years ago, the only way to market your property was by trying to sell it yourself or hire a real estate agent to do much of the work for you. Today, there are more buying and selling options. Buy Owner, Help-U-Sell and other independent real estate agents can be found who charge a nominal fee to list your home on the Multiple Listing Service (MLS). They do not charge five to seven percent of the sale price of your home like a traditional realtor, but they also do little more than place your home on the MLS and leave you with much of the actual selling responsibility. You may want to consider this route initially to try and save yourself from paying a large commission, but fully research all independent selling options before you decide which one to use. The internet can help you with your investigation.

In most cases, I strongly caution against trying to sell your house yourself because you really need to know whether a potential buyer is financially qualified and even if they are seriously interested in purchasing a house. You do not want to open your home to complete strangers who are merely nosey or are possibly only interested in your decorating ideas and floor plan. Unfortunately, there could even be unsavory types touring your home who are "staking out" properties as they plan their next burglary. The contents and layout of your home could be rather enticing to such a person. Many kinds of people exist with many objectives in mind.

A good realtor will screen the unwelcome types who have the wrong intentions and help secure your property as much as possible. Keep in mind, that realtors provide this service for a living so they should do the job properly. In addition, and most importantly, a professionally licensed real estate agent has the necessary experience, knowledge, and contacts to work for you to sell your property as efficiently and effectively as possible. They should know how to prepare your home, price it properly, present it, market it, complete all necessary documents, assist in helping potential buyers obtain financing, if necessary, and facilitate the process from earliest inception to successful conclusion.

- Investigate the various ways to market your property.

- Research and evaluate the marketing conditions in your area and neighborhood.

- Review your finances and consider the cost of a realtor's commission.

- Decide to sell it yourself, hire a realtor or use an independent agency.

5 | Selecting a Real Estate Agent

As you are probably aware, there is virtually an endless supply of realtors across the United States. We see advertisements in the newspapers, in our mail, on the web and even on billboards and radio stations in some areas. How do you find the realtor that is best suited to meet your needs? When I am ready to sell, I always begin by recalling the experience I had with the agent whose services I most recently used. Was I satisfied with the job he/she did for me? If I have positive memories of that interaction, I definitely put him/her on my list of possible selling agents to consider. If I was displeased with the job he/she did, that person is eliminated. Next, I ask friends and neighbors for their recommendations. They are often your best source because they will usually happily and honestly tell you about their positive and negative real estate dealings. Also, check out local listings, real estate websites and your newspaper's weekend real estate section to familiarize yourself with possible agents and agencies.

I strongly advise you to think seriously before enlisting the services of a close friend or family member in the real estate business. I say this because it is much easier to fire an unsatisfactory agent you are not connected to, but it is nearly impossible to confront or dismiss an inadequate realtor who is also your good friend or relative without causing pain to all parties.

In addition, disclosure of personal financial information is usually required during real estate transactions. You may not feel comfortable sharing these private details with friends and family. Remember your home is usually your largest investment and you want this process handled with the utmost of professionalism. This business relationship is much too important to have it in the hands of someone with whom you have emotional and or familial attachments. The old adage which suggests avoiding mixing business with pleasure especially holds true under these circumstances.

Once you have gathered enough prospective names, it is time to phone each realtor and schedule appointments to meet them at your home. I suggest you schedule meetings with at least three agents, preferably from three separate agencies. I urge you to look at representatives from several companies because each has a different style, idea, standard and marketing strategy. For example, there may be a small locally run agency that can provide you and your home with lots of personal attention, but lacks broad networking capabilities. A huge nationally known company might not offer enough of a personal touch, but their name recognition and large market share could give your property more wide spread exposure. Another alternative is an agency which employs agents that work as individuals under a large company umbrella, granting them more flexibility to work with you in a manner perhaps more suitable to both of you. Only you can decide which approach is most appropriate for you.

Now, take time to carefully interview each agent and determine which one you will hire to do the important job of marketing your valuable asset. Gather whatever paperwork you have pertaining to your house to refer to if the need arises during the interviews. It is likely you will need to refer to the property title, warranty deed, property survey, recent property tax statement and closing documents. Do not rush the interview process. Start by giving the agent a complete tour of your home. Be sure to point out any unique or special features in each room and open every closet and storage area. Perhaps your home has architectural enhancements or upscale accessories that add to its value and appeal. Let the agent know about any and all improvements you have made since you first purchased your home. If you have built on an addition, finished a terrace or basement level, installed custom window treatments, upgraded interior or exterior materials and/or replaced an outdated kitchen or bathroom, be sure to provide details including the costs of these projects since these changes will likely add substantial value and appreciation to your property.

Next, you should present a list of questions you have prepared in advance to each perspective agent. Here is a sampling of suggested questions and explanations presented in no particular order. Do not limit yourself to this list because you may have additional questions that are suitable for your particular property and situation. It is crucial that you and your agent establish expectations before agreeing to work together.

What is your level of experience selling real estate?

How many transactions have you personally been involved in during the past year? How many have you listed and how many have you sold? Some agents accumulate listings so they are guaranteed a piece of the commission, but do little to actually sell the houses. In other words, some agents specialize in listings and others in actually selling. You want to know that your agent will work with you from beginning to end. It is important to know that the agent has a successful track record.

How do you plan to market my property?

Will you present my home on the Multiple Listing Service? Will you print and distribute brochures and mass mailings? Will you advertise my home on local television and in the newspapers and magazines? Will you hold public and broker open houses? Do you plan to list my property on the internet with a virtual tour? Will you use referral resources and promote my property to other real estate professionals? Ask for samples of their media work.

How long do you think it will take to sell my property?

Ask in terms of weeks or months and ask for reasons to back up their estimated time frame. The current market conditions will help the agent estimate the probable time involved to produce a successful sale. If you are in a rush to sell, the marketing tactics and listing price will probably be altered.

What if anything, do I need to do to further improve the marketability of my house?

You should have already done a lot of preparation work prior to this meeting, but you may have overlooked something. Double check that everything is in good working order. You do not want the door knob to fall off as the homebuyer opens the front door!

What would you like me to do to help present the property prior to a showing?

Often you, your family and your pets will be asked to leave for a showing to avoid the discomfort associated with a stranger examining your home. Before you leave you must tidy up every-thing, everywhere. Remove and/or hide all small valuables such as jewelry and cash to avoid any possible theft. Realtors usually want you to put lights on, empty trash baskets, make beds, open all window blinds, wash the dishes, freshly vacuum and store any clutter such as stacks of mail. Some may even suggest turning on soft music, putting a fire in the fireplace (if available and seasonally appropriate), freshening the air with potpourri or room deodorizer and adding fresh flowers to the décor. I have even placed a fountain near the front door to mask noise from a nearby road. My dear mother often placed refrigerated cookie dough in the oven to give the house a "homey" fragrance. Baking an apple pie might even be a better idea since it cooks longer and creates a pleasant scent that will linger for hours. Selling a home is a lot of work and is disruptive to your life, but these special touches and attention to detail will help hasten the sale of your property and turn your house into a "show place." The candidate agents you interview may offer other suggestions appropriate for your specific home.

What should the asking price be?
 How did you determine that figure?

This question is probably the most important one on the list. The agent should come to your meeting prepared with comparable listings and recent sales in your vicinity. If your home is priced too high, there will be fewer qualified buyers viewing your property and it will take longer to sell. Savvy agents and buyers are usually turned off by homes that are overpriced. Even if you are offered a higher price, the property may not appraise at the level needed for the buyer to obtain a mortgage. An appraisal is an evaluation of the property usually determined by a professional hired by a lending institution or bank to assess dollar value in the current real estate marketplace. Mortgage lenders will require an appraisal prior to granting a mortgage. Pricing your residence below market value will usually result in a quick sale, but does not give you what your home is truly worth, resulting in less cash in your pocket. Strategize with the agents to come up with an acceptable listing price within a reasonable market range for your home. It is probably wise to set the initial price slightly higher than where you want to end up so that you have a bit of negotiating space, but not too much to discourage prospective buyers. Be very careful when pricing your property because having to reduce the price later may reflect negatively on your home. Think about the time value of money and remember the longer your home sits on the market, the more mortgage and taxes you will pay.

What are the terms of the listing agreement?

Ask for a sample copy of the listing contract so you can carefully review it at your convenience. If you want clarification on anything or have questions, ask until you fully understand everything. Most real estate companies ask for a time commitment ranging from three to six months. Negotiate for the shortest term so the realtors know they must do their job as quickly and effectively as possible or they will lose your business.

Can the agreement be canceled if I become dissatisfied with your service?

Many realty companies will not allow clients to cancel a listing contract because they view the agreement as a binding contract. If there is an addendum to nullify the agreement, you usually pay penalty fees. Find out about all these details before signing anything. With one of my homes, I fired an unproductive agent through an escape clause because he brought no offers after several months. I then hired a new agent who marketed the house much more aggressively and it sold in a few weeks.

Will you personally show my property?

Unfortunately, some agents are more interested in securing your listing to guarantee themselves a percentage of the commission check than in actually doing the bulk of the work. You only want an agent who is willing to work for you and do the entire job. It may be difficult for your agent to be at each and every requested showing, but he can send a trusted representative in his place. Your agent should at least place a lock box containing the key to your house on or near your front door. The key can only be obtained through a changeable code, accessible by only licensed real estate agents. This device allows him or her to closely monitor who has been in to view your property. Data on the agents who show the house is electronically recorded, giving your agent the ability to follow-up and get feedback.

Will you place a sign in my front yard and will your phone number be the posted contact number?

Some homeowner associations prohibit posting any advertising signage on your property. If you live in an area without this restriction, it is wise to have a "for sale" sign installed in the most visible part of your yard. If you reside on a corner lot, you may require two signs, one for each side street, so a sign can be seen from both directions. I lived on a private drive with no outlet, so my agent placed a sign at the very end of the roadway and another directly on my front lawn. Consider the location of your lot and discuss sign placement in advance. Real estate agents have told me that as many as fifteen percent of homebuyers initially identified the house they ultimately purchased by seeing a sign on a property and calling the number displayed. Be sure the number is one that reaches your agent quickly and does not merely go into a voice mail system. Timing and communication is crucial when you have an interested buyer.

What will you do to help secure my property?

For your peace of mind, you must feel confident that your agent is going to do his/her best to protect your valuable assets. He/she is entrusted to only allow access to your home to serious, qualified buyers who are accompanied by a realtor. Agents must "keep an eye" on all clients by closely escorting them throughout your entire home. Your home must also be locked up to your specifications when a showing is completed. If you have an alarm system and wish to have it reset after a viewing, you must give the realtor careful operational instructions.

How will you deal with my pet(s)?

Usually it is best to take dogs and cats with you during a showing, if possible. No need to worry about the goldfish or parakeet! In the event you are unable to take Spot or Kitty, discuss the best possible alternative with the realtor candidate. My cat, filled with fright, huddled under my bed during showings so he was no trouble. My dog was usually content on her bed which I placed in the garage with a treat and toy before I left. If you have an overly friendly, aggressive or potentially destructive pet, place the animal in a crate whenever you must leave it. You do not want your pet to jump on people, bite people, chew the furniture or use your house as a toilet. Sometimes a crate is the only alternative.

What is your commission structure and is it negotiable?

The answer to the second part of this question is almost always yes. Of course the agent will not generally offer a reduction in the commission rate unless you ask for it. This is of great importance to both parties because agents earn their living from commissions and you pay for their services through the commission. Most agreements stipulate that six or even seven percent of the sale price is payable to the real estate agent(s) at the time the sale closes. Three or three and one half percent goes to the listing agency and the same amount goes to the selling agency. For example, if you list with Re/Max and Century 21 brings the buyer, they split the total commission. If the agency you select to sell your home also produces the buyer, the agency gets the entire six or seven percent. The agency or agencies involved keep another percentage and then the realtors get their share. You should certainly have some commission negotiating room if the agency performs well on both sides of the deal. In this event, they will receive double the typical funds and get the entire commission. If the house sells very quickly, the realtors do less work and spend less money on advertising. You may be able to negotiate to have the contract stipulate a lower commission if the house sells within a short period of time. For example, maybe you can get them to agree to a five percent commission if the house is under contract within thirty days. Perhaps you can even get the realtor to agree to a lower commission if he or she sells the house themselves with no other agent involvement. In this case the realtor does not share the realtor portion with anyone and enjoys a large payday at closing. I have usually been able to negotiate for one percentage point below the usual terms if the house sells quickly and two percentage points lower if the agent I hire also brings the buyer and sells my property him/herself. Be sure to put the results of any commission negotiations in writing in the listing contract before signing on the dotted line.

Ask for several references to make inquiries of past clients.

If there is any hesitation here, you should cross this agent off your candidate list. Take the time to phone these people and do your best to get their honest opinions. Ask for specifics and examples to back up their viewpoints. Ask if they would rehire the agent if they needed to sell again.

Will you provide me with frequent updates and prompt showing feedback?

Communication is very important as you both proceed as a team to market and sell your property. Your realtor should agree to speak with you at least twice a week, to keep you informed on the progress of your sale. You should feel comfortable contacting your agent whenever you need to ask a question or discuss a concern. Sometimes you just need to know you can share your thoughts and frustrations with your agent to help you relax during the sometimes stressful days of marketing your home.

How would you advise me to handle a purchase offer that is below my asking price?

Interested parties will sometimes present an extremely low offer in an attempt to get a bargain basement price. A quality agent will assist you as you determine whether to remain firm with your price or answer the bid with a counteroffer. It is important to discuss negotiating tactics in advance in the event you are faced with a possible buyer who wants to negotiate. Most buyers do want to negotiate. In fact homes typically sell for a bit less than the asking price, but you should feel confident that your realtor will have your goals in mind while trying to close the best possible deal.

Can your agency provide any relocation services?

Your real estate broker may be able to refer you to a competent agent in your new location and suggest mortgage brokers, closing attorneys and even reputable moving companies. You can at least begin that research with a little help from your realtor. More about these steps later.

Upon completion of the interview stage, carefully review the responses you received from each agent to determine your level of satisfaction from each one. Did you find their answers acceptable or unacceptable and which questions do you feel are most important? I also encourage you to pay attention to your instincts when evaluating your level of comfort with each prospective broker. Who do you feel is most honorable, trustworthy, reliable and capable? Approach this interview process with the same mindset you used to decide whether or not to move. Weigh all the pros and cons until you reach a satisfactory conclusion.

Invite the most impressive realtor back, get the necessary paperwork filled out, signed and copied. You will need to have your property deed or title, survey and tax statement available for the realtor to copy for his/her records. Some of this information is included in the actual listing. The title or deed provides legal evidence of ownership of the property. The survey or drawing of the lot includes the dimensions and square footage of your property. The tax statement provides government identification and tax obligations for your property. You will have to complete and sign a residential listing contract and probably a property disclosure form. You will also want to list inclusions and exclusions on this contract. Inclusions are those items that will remain with your home when you vacate the property. Appliances and anything securely attached to the structure such as light fixtures are usually included. If you want to take Grandma's antique chandelier to your new residence along with your nearly new washer and dryer, be sure to specify these items as exclusions or replace them prior to any showings.

Some states require owners to disclose to a possible buyer all known facts that may adversely affect the value of a property that may not be readily observable. Some states have brief and fairly simple forms that take only minutes to fill out and sign. Others, such as California require homeowners to fill out lengthy questionnaires requesting very detailed information. For example, you might be asked to identify any problems you have knowledge of concerning the condition of the roof, the plumbing, the electrical system, the heating and cooling systems and even the appliances. More complex questions might include specific details about your home and even neighborhood. One disclosure I filled out even wanted to know whether anyone had ever died in the house. Your newly hired agent should slowly walk you through this paperwork to make sure all is filled out completely and correctly. Feel free to ask questions so you completely understand what you are signing. You are now ready to proceed with the marketing of your property.

- Begin to search for possible realtor candidates.

- Make appointments with three highly recommended prospective real estate agents.

- Gather all paperwork pertinent to your home, i.e., title, deed, closing documents, etc.

- Interview each agent using questions and suggestions found in chapter five.

- Make careful notes during each interview.

- Review the responses and suggestions from each candidate's interview.

- Invite the most impressive agent back to discuss every listing detail.

- Complete all necessary listing documents and disclosure forms.

6 | Let the Showings Begin

Now that the house is listed it is time to open your home to as many potential buyers as possible. It is crucial that you and your family cooperate by keeping the house tidy and by making your home available whenever it accommodates the schedules of the buyers and their agents. As I mentioned earlier, it is best to leave the premises during a showing because it can be uncomfortable having strangers in your home. While marketing my home in New Jersey, a couple came with their parents and the mother remarked, "This ghastly wall paper must go the minute you move in!" I was very offended because I had just recently finished putting up the wall covering and thought it was very attractive. After that, I left whenever possible to avoid such discomfort. Don't feel you should remain at home in the event the house hunters have any questions. It is always best to have all questions filtered through your agent who has your best interests in mind. If your agent has done his/her homework, he/she usually knows the proper response to shoppers' questions based on experience and the information gathered from you.

It is possible that you will have to allow a showing on a

moment's notice. You might be in the midst of preparing dinner, have a sick child in bed, or maybe you just stepped out of the shower! Try to handle these circumstances with humor. I had my father-in-law over for lunch when I got a call that a serious buyer had seen the sign in my yard and wanted to view the house in a mere ten minutes. In this situation, it was impossible to leave, so we quickly scrambled to pick up the children's toys, straightened the kitchen, placed the little ones in angelic poses, put smiles on our faces and let the showing proceed. Surprisingly, an acceptable offer came through a few hours later. A friend of mine got a call from a realtor wanting to show her home during a New England blizzard. Her children were home from school due to the weather, so the home was not at its best! She was tempted to say it was not a good time to show it, but she agreed despite her misgivings and an acceptable offer came in that evening. She later learned that the husband had already previewed the property and wanted his wife to see it. She was only in town that one day to look at houses. Remember, it may seem like the wrong time for you, but it just might be the correct time for the buyer. You never know when the "right buyer" may come to your door.

I did not think I would bring religion or superstition into this handbook, but I feel I might be remiss if I did not mention the legend of Saint Joseph. Saint Joseph is the patron saint of the home and believers feel he has helped them sell their houses. The Urban Legend website tells the tale of how burying a statue of Saint Joseph in the front yard facing the house will help sell your house quickly. Some believe the statues should be placed in a position of respect such as on top of the mantel. This legend is well known throughout the real estate community. The statues are usually available in Christian bookstores. I have actually followed the faithful by burying Saint Joseph at two of my homes that we were very anxious to sell. The buyers came soon afterwards. I'm not sure if the statue had anything to do with the selling of the houses, but I am certain that the good saint did no harm. I recommend doing whatever you feel will help you.

Try to remain patient, optimistic and cooperative during this stressful time. Some house hunters find the ideal house for them in just one visit and make an offer after just one visit. Others feel the need to see the home numerous times and bring friends, relatives and even measuring tapes to help them determine whether a house is right for them. I know this all feels intrusive and uncomfortable, but this is often part of this step. Communicate frequently with your realtor and continue to enjoy your current home. Remember it is imperative to keep up with all your domestic duties. Trust me, your home will sell. I wish you multiple offers in minimal time!

- Keep your house clean and tidy so you are prepared for a short notice showing.

- Accommodate the schedules of agents and potential buyers.

- Communicate frequently with your agent to obtain feedback from showings.

- Follow the suggestions offered by your realtor if further changes need to be made.

- Remain optimistic, cooperative and patient.

7 | Before the SOLD Sign

Your realtor gives you the good news that an offer has been presented on your home. Carefully go over the sales contract offer and determine if everything mentioned is acceptable to you and your family. The buyer should have examined your home and carefully reviewed your disclosure papers prior to writing an offer enabling him/her to become very familiar with your home. This contract is a legal agreement between you and the buyer which explains in detail, exactly what the purchase includes, when the buyer can move in, what guarantees exist, when the closing or settlement will take place and what recourse exists for both parties if the contract is not fulfilled. The buyer will include a deposit or binder of at least $1000 as earnest money and then promise to make an additional deposit within a few days if you decide to accept their offer. The binder funds are held in an escrow account to lock in the right to purchase a home according to the terms agreed upon by both parties. An escrow account is a holding place for documents and funds managed by a third party on behalf of the buyer and seller until all conditions of the purchase agreement are met. These escrow funds are usually held in an interest bearing, insured bank account, where they will remain until the property closing takes place. The deposit provides the seller with a bit of protection by demonstrating the seriousness on the part of the buyer to complete the transaction.

Closely examine all terms specified in the sales contract prior to accepting the offer. I don't recommend losing a sale because the buyer requests you to include the refrigerator you had excluded or the bar stools painted to match the kitchen's specific décor. It is fairly easy to replace these items and usually not worth the extra aggravation of prolonging the marketing time. Sometimes the requested closing date is a potential problem. A friend of mine was presented an offer that requested her to vacate the property and close in ten days. This request would have caused the family too much hardship because the children were in school and they had no where yet to go. The potential buyer would not negotiate a different date so the deal failed to materialize. Do not feel bad for my friend because a more reasonable person made an acceptable offer within two weeks. Offers that include such pressure tactics are often accompanied by low prices and are not to be taken too seriously.

Of course, some buyers make very low offers just to try to get a great deal. I have had this happen to me several times and have learned that unless they are willing to offer a somewhat fair price and negotiate with you, they are probably just playing a game and are not serious about purchasing your home. Don't feel insulted by low offers; just be aware there are those people who are only looking for a bargain. I assure the "right buyer" will eventually come through your front door.

Keep in mind that you may need to be a bit flexible as you contemplate any offer made on your property. It is unwise to walk away from an offer if most of your stipulations have been met. I agreed to a contract that offered less money than I really wanted for my house because my husband had already left to begin his new job, and we decided it was not worth a few thousand dollars to continue being apart until "maybe" a better offer came along. We figured it could have been another month or two or even longer before someone else presented another offer. Also, the market had been a bit slow, the rest of the terms were reasonable and we were not willing to wait any longer to have our family back together. Utilize the advice and skills of your realtor as you decide whether to accept, reject or counter an offer. Usually, if the buyer is serious, most things are negotiable and compromises can be made by both parties. I hope your first offer is a good one that becomes a sales contract agreed to by all involved.

It is great to have a signed contract in hand, but you still need to hold off on your celebration until you learn that all terms of the contract have been met. Most importantly, the buyers must prove they have the funds necessary to close the deal. A signed letter from a lender guaranteeing a mortgage to the buyer is real plus and makes an offer very attractive. Some buyers will want the agreement contingent upon the sale of another property they own. They may need the monies from another home to afford to close on your home. I encourage you to avoid this type of agreement and suggest you require the buyer to obtain a temporary loan, called a bridge loan, which allows them to close in a timely manner. If they do not sell their home quickly and they have no bridge loan, you will then (unless you can carry the financial burden of two homes) be forced to delay your plans until they sell their home. The only time I would consider accepting this type of arrangement is if your home has been for sale for over three months and there have been no other promising offers, and/or the buyer allows you to continue showing your property while they are waiting to sell theirs. This way you have the opportunity to protect your interests and accept another bid in the event one comes along. You are obligated to inform the first buyer when another offer is presented and grant them the opportunity to make their initial bid more attractive or withdraw the offer and lose the house to the new buyer. This practice is referred to as "right of first refusal."

Purchase agreements should usually only be contingent upon the results of a home inspection and a mortgage approval. Many buyers in today's marketplace will have a letter of mortgage approval prior to presenting an offer. In this case the contract should not be held up by anything other than inspections. Seldom will a buyer purchase a home without ordering a thorough home inspection and a pest inspection. It is probably even more infrequent for a buyer to possess the cash to buy the house and not require some sort of financing. Only once in all my moves did I have the dream buyer who required no financing and requested no inspections. That is what I call a squeaky clean deal not to be refused!

While you are waiting for positive news to proceed with the sale, your home is considered a pending sale. As I mentioned earlier, insist that your agent continue to market and show your property until all contingencies are lifted. It is still possible that the agreement could dissolve if problems arise with financing or an inspector writes a negative report which reveals defects beyond the expected such as major termite damage or faulty wiring. This is why I urged you in chapter three to pay for an inspection before listing your home in order to prevent this possible setback. If the buyer simply decides he/she no longer wants the house or his/her plans change, you should be able to claim the buyer's deposit money which should be held in an escrow account. These monies are designed to compensate the seller for any inconveniences resulting from a faulty contract. Sometimes a sticker is placed on the yard sign to indicate that a sale is in process. Other times the sign remains unchanged until the deal is finalized and a "sold" sign is exhibited. Discuss this matter with your realtor. I suggest you wait for the "sold" sign since a "pending sale" or "under contract" notice may discourage other potential buyers from viewing your property. You want others to consider your house in the event your intended deal falls apart.

Generally a home inspection occurs within a week after the purchase agreement is accepted by the seller. The buyer hires and pays a professional engineer who is also a licensed inspector to closely examine the structural and operational condition of your house to help them determine whether the property is a worthy investment. They are not there to evaluate the cosmetic condition of the home. The seller must make the home available for an inspection if requested by the buyer. The appointment is usually attended by the buyer too and can last for as long as several hours depending on the size of your residence. It is very unusual for a house to pass the stringent tests and examining eyes of a diligent inspector with flying colors, so do not be upset if the inspector points out minor infractions. I have had reports of squeaky doors and even a screw missing from a door hinge. In fact, inspectors usually find imperfections of which sellers are completely unaware. Brand new homes often have numerous faults as well. If the inspector finds major problems such as a weak foundation, leaking roof, potentially hazardous conditions, or significant termite damage, the buyer can legally back out of the deal and have all their deposit money refunded as per the inspection contingency. They also have the right to cancel the contract if a problem arises with the title search or if they believe the property was misrepresented within the disclosure forms.

Fortunately, most inspection reports cite only small infractions which can be easily and inexpensively corrected. Buyers are almost always content when the seller agrees to repair or replace any troubles mentioned in the inspector's report. Sometimes you must hire professionals to fix the small problems and give copies of the receipts to the buyer's agent proving the work was successfully completed. Keep these records in case they are needed at the time of settlement. I had to have a chimney cleaned following an inspection and my realtor gave the buyer's realtor the necessary paperwork showing that the service had been performed. Do not be shocked if the inspection report comes back with a lengthy list of needed repairs. Inspectors are paid to find fault with your home. You may agree or disagree with the items put in the report, but you must address each and every one regardless of your feelings in order to close the deal. You may have the right to obtain estimates for completing all mentioned infractions and offer a cash value in lieu of dealing with all the repairs while you are residing in the house. A family I know chose not to replace a large window with a broken seal and offered to pay the buyers the estimated cost of the repair so that the closing would not be delayed. The buyers accepted the cash and the realtors documented the transaction as part of the property transfer.

The other significant contingency to the sale is that the buyer must obtain any necessary financing within the period of time specified in the purchase agreement. Usually the buyer has five business days to apply for a new mortgage loan or prove they have the means to take over making payments to your existing loan (assume your home loan). A loan commitment must be obtained in a reasonable amount of time (approximately thirty days) and the buyer must show reasonable effort to obtain the funds. Your realtor should check on the progress of the loan application and all other open contingencies to make sure the deal is moving forward towards closure. Remember it is best to have a letter from a lender granting a loan to the buyer prior to agreeing to a contract of sale to avoid mortgage troubles and setbacks.

I wish you smooth sailing as you proceed from offer to pending sale to closure. Keep in mind this stage is often or mostly trouble free and can even be educational!

- Examine all terms specified in the contracted offer.

- Decide whether you will accept or reject the offer as written.

- Write a counter offer with changes, if appropriate.

- Negotiate, if necessary, until you and the buyer agree on all terms.

- Obtain a copy of the buyer's loan approval.

- Meet with buyer's inspector(s) when they examine your property.

- Make all reasonable corrections pointed out in the inspectors' reports.

- Keep proof of all repairs and costs with your other property documents.

8 | Securing a Mortgage or Lease

The purpose of this chapter is to provide you with basic knowledge concerning mortgages and leases. A mortgage is a loan contract in which the borrower's (buyer) property is pledged as collateral to be repaid in installments over a number of years. The buyer promises to repay the principal (the amount of money borrowed) and interest on that principal. The homeowner must also pay for property insurance, all taxes and maintenance costs. A lease is a legal contract granting use or occupation of a property during a specified period of time in exchange for a specified rental fee. I believe it is important to educate yourself about mortgages and leases prior to shopping for your new residence so that you can determine whether you want to buy or lease and how and what you are capable of spending. If you do not take adequate time to research what you can truly afford, you could become very disappointed if you fall in love with a house, condominium or apartment you are not qualified to pay for or buy. I am not pretending to be a banker, financier or mortgage broker, but as a frequent house shopper, I have picked up some valuable information to share with you in simple language that even I can comprehend. I have purchased eight houses and one condominium, leased three apartments and helped my daughter search for apartments several times, so I am well aware of the financial requirements for both renting and buying.

It is wise to begin by checking your credit rating or FICO score for accuracies prior to hunting for your new home. FICO is the acronym for Fair Isaac Corporation, the firm that developed the scoring model used by the three major credit bureaus. The three main bureaus are Trans Union, Equifax and Experian. In fact, the moment you decide to relocate would be the perfect time to learn your credit score and examine your credit report. Creditors can take weeks or even months to eliminate or correct mistakes you discover in your report. Obviously, the sooner you research your score and report, the better. It is crucial to have your report as accurate and strong as possible because the healthier your credit rating, the easier it will be for you to get a loan. In some cases it will determine your loan rate. The better you score, the better your mortgage rate. I guarantee every potential lender or leasing company will access your credit information to determine whether or not to grant you a mortgage or allow you to rent property. You may have finished school a long time ago, but you still have a "report card" in the form of a credit evaluation.

Fortunately, the three main bureaus have recently joined forces to create one national clearing house which makes it easier for consumers to access their credit scores and reports. Your credit rating is calculated based on information that compares your payment history to the information on the reports of thousands of other customers. Your score is used to help determine how deserving you are of obtaining a loan. FICO refuses to release details about what spending and debt behavior it looks for in calculating credit scores. All the bureau will say is that you should pay bills promptly and use your credit wisely. FICO scores range from 300 to 900. The average score nationally is 677. If you score is above 800, your score is outstanding because the chance that you will be delinquent with a payment is 1 in 1,292. If it is 700 or more, you should be able to get a loan and the likelihood that you will be remiss with payment is about 1 in 123. If your score is less than 600, there is probably trouble indicated on your report and you'll have difficulty borrowing money. The chance that you will not meet your financial obligations becomes 1 in 8. If your score rates you in the 500s, you will not get a mortgage or lease. Basically, the higher your number, the more likely you are to obtain a mortgage or lease because you are considered low risk to the lender. Late payments, bankruptcies and delinquencies all damage credit scores. Also, if you already have excessive debt or have recently applied for several loans, your score will probably decline. Obviously keeping your report as healthy and accurate as possible is very important. Your score improves when you pay all your bills on time, pay off as much debt as possible and do not open any new credit accounts just prior to applying for a mortgage or lease. If you have children, educate them as they enter their teens about personal finances so they know the ramifications of their credit histories too.

You can obtain your credit report from several online sites simply by going to almost any search engine and typing in "credit report". You can also go to www.annualcreditreport.com to find your information or you may phone 877–322–8228. You might want to consider requesting your credit reports from all three privately held companies because they compile their information in slightly different ways. Contact Equifax at www.Equifax.com or 1–800–685–1111, Experian at www.Experian.com or 1–800–888–4213 and TransUnion at www.Transunion.com or 1–800–422–4879. Probably the easiest way to get all three of your scores and reports is by going to the Fair Isaac site at www.myfico.com. There may be a fee charged for a thorough report, but this is in the process of being eliminated due to a new federal law passed in 2005 requiring the big three credit reporting agencies to offer consumers at least one free report annually. Some states already have similar laws in place. Georgia, for example gives residents the right to obtain two free reports each year. Research the law in your state and even if you have to pay to access this personal data, it can be invaluable to you, especially if you uncover mistakes.

After you have determined your credit worthiness, you need to determine the monthly loan or rental fee you are capable of and willing to pay. Some people choose to take a conservative approach when it comes to their housing expenses while others are willing to spend a larger portion of their income to live in luxury. Whatever avenue you take is a matter of personality, comfort level and priorities. Only you know what is best for you and your situation. My parents always selected comfortable yet modest homes even though they could afford more extravagant accommodations, because they had fairly simple tastes and always dreamed of early retirement and extensive travel. I have other relatives who prefer lavish homes and are willing to pay the price for a "show place" while foregoing other extras. Only you know your goals and priorities and what is best for your own situation.

The mortgage and leasing industry will help you determine what you can afford because they use basic formulas to evaluate what amount you are capable of repaying. This is called the housing expense-to-income ratio. The standard formula suggests housing expenses not exceed 28% of your gross income. For example, if your total gross (before income taxes) annual household income is $50,000, your gross income is $4,166.66 each month. Traditional industry guidelines allow you to spend no more than $1,166.66 per month on total housing payments.

The housing payment for rental property is usually the rental fee and possibly an additional cost for parking privileges.

A mortgage payment includes four major components which are referred to as PITI or principle, interest, taxes and insurance. The principle is the monthly amount paid over the life of the loan to repay the money borrowed. The interest is the cost paid by the borrower to use the loaned money. Shopping for the lowest interest rate is important because the lower the interest rate, the lower the total mortgage payment. For example a 6% interest rate on a $100,000 thirty year conventional mortgage will cost $599.56 per month. An 8% rate will cost $733.77 each month and a 10% rate will cost $877.57 per month. For more detailed information on mortgages visit www.mortgage.com and/or www.realtor.com and select the mortgage calculator to accurately estimate monthly mortgage payments.

Your monthly house payment will almost always include your property taxes and insurance. Some people prefer to exclude these fees from their monthly payment and pay them directly to their local government or insurance agency instead of through their lender. Look into your options and decide what works best for your budget. Taxes are the fees assessed on a property based on a value determined by a local taxing authority. Local governments use these dollars to pay for community services and schools. Insurance is another portion of a mortgage payment required by every lender to cover the home in the event of damage to the property. The insurance protects both the lender and the homeowner if a calamity occurs. If a purchaser makes a down payment of less than 20% of the home's price, there is often an additional fee tacked onto the PITI to pay for mortgage insurance. Financing 80% or less helps to keep your payment down by eliminating the need for mortgage insurance.

The mortgage industry also strongly considers a potential

customer's revenues and assets as well as what is known as long term debt-to-income ratio when deciding whether or not to grant a mortgage. Long term debts are fixed payments that span twelve months or more. Alimony, child support, vehicle leases or loans, educational debts, credit card debt and any large purchase loans such as furniture credit plans fall into this classification. Some condominiums and neighborhoods have association fees or property maintenance fees which would also be considered part of this category. It is vital for you to list all of your debts to establish what you can truly afford to pay for housing. Be honest with yourself as you go through this evaluation process. Over estimate personal expenses if necessary so you do not end up financially strapped. If you are able to pay off some of your long term debt prior to applying for a mortgage, you will qualify for a larger loan. A mortgage application is likely to be declined if fixed expenditures exceed 36% of total gross income. In other words, if you bring in $50,000 annually, and $4,1666.66 monthly, your total debts including housing payments should be less than or equal to $1,499.99 each month.

Whether you agree with the qualifying formulas or not, the lending business has vast experience to back up these numbers. There might be some flexibility within these general rules based upon your specific financial circumstances and credit reports, but sticking to this math is usually advisable. When you consider all your daily living costs, you will realize that these guidelines seem quite sensible. Besides housing and your usual debt payments, a big chunk of your salary goes to pay federal, local, social security, state (with a few exceptions), property and sales taxes. Of course you have food, utilities, clothing, gasoline or transportation, insurance policies and leisure activities to budget for too. Life is expensive! If you allocate too much for housing, you will become "house poor" and have few discretionary dollars to spend. I assure you that would not be a desirable lifestyle. My husband and I lived under those circumstances when we purchased our first home and we went two years without vacations, dinners out or any new clothes. That was not much fun!

Here is a sample exercise to clarify what I have presented:

Gross Annual Income - $50,000.00

Gross Monthly Income - $4,166.66

Housing Expense-to-Income Ratio of 28% - $1,166.66

Long Term Debt-to-Income Ratio of 36% - $1,499.99

For the purpose of this example, let's assume an applicant has a four year car loan, five years to repay a college debt and pays a major credit card company at least $50 each month. The applicant's long term debt would look like this:

Monthly auto payment - $225.00

Monthly college loan - $75.00

Monthly credit payment - *$50.00*

Total $350.00

Long Term Debt-to-Income Ratio (36%) $1,499.99

Subtract long term debt - *$350.00*

Total left for housing payment $1,149.00

Now get out your calculator and insert all your figures to come up with the amount you can truly afford to spend on your next residence. If you are planning to buy a home, the more cash you have for a down payment, the less you will have to borrow. The down payment is the difference between the selling price and the amount mortgaged. The down payment is paid in full at the time the deal closes. As I mentioned earlier in this chapter, if you put down 20% or more of the purchase price, you shouldn't have to pay for mortgage insurance. This alone can lower your total mortgage payment by almost $100.00 each month.

You also need to be aware of the fact that you will need cash on hand to pay for closing costs as both the seller of your old property and the buyer of your new property. Closing costs are all the fees paid at the time of settlement associated with obtaining a mortgage loan and transferring a real estate title. These expenses vary greatly from state to state, so be sure to get a "good faith estimate" of the fees well in advance so you are spared a jaw-dropping experience at the last minute. We shockingly discovered we owed the State of New York over $10,000 in seller's costs when we sold our house there. This happened to be a state tax undisclosed to us until the day before closing. We had to quickly shuffle money around and change a few plans to pay this additional fee. Insist that your real estate agent and lender provide you with all accurate figures so you avoid similar unpleasant surprises! I will discuss more details concerning real estate closings in a later chapter. Just be aware that you have much financial planning to do when making housing decisions.

Mortgage interest rates are also an important part of your financial planning. The rate you obtain will impact how much you can affordably borrow. The lower the rate, the lower your monthly payment and vise versa. You can find current rates from various lenders in the business section of daily newspapers and online. Obviously, you want to find the best (lowest) rate you possibly can with the most favorable terms for your needs. If you can lock in a rate, that is even better. Locking in will enable you to keep the same rate you qualified for at the time of application until you close on your next home. There may be a fee associated with locking in, but if rates are predicted to increase, the money may be well spent. At the time I began writing this book, interest rates on a fixed thirty year mortgage were, and fortunately still are, at the lowest levels seen in decades. As of March 7, 2007 an individual with a strong credit score can find a conventional fixed rate thirty year mortgage for approximately 6%. E-loan.com can help you quickly find daily lending rates. This is almost unbelievable to me, because the best rate my husband and I found while purchasing our first home in 1982 was 17%! I am thrilled and excited for the many more families who can now achieve the American dream of owning their own home!

I hope this chapter helps you understand the financing basics. For more precise and elaborate information, you must contact a mortgage expert. The Fannie Mae Foundation, a non-profit organization, offers several free booklets to help buyers learn more details about mortgage plans and options. These booklets help educate the first-time buyer and provide a beneficial review for everyone else. They contain information on everything from loan types and options to a detailed mortgage qualification worksheet. Even the nosey questions lenders ask are detailed in these booklets. Their website is www.homebuyingguide.com. You can also contact Fannie Mae at 1-800-611-9566. There are so many financing options today because lenders are trying to satisfy the diverse requirements of their many customers. Thirty year and fifteen year fixed rate loans, adjustable rate loans in which interest rates are adjusted annually according to the changes in the financial market, balloon loans with lower payments for the early years of the loan and then increased payments in later years, and even zero down payment loans and interest only loans are all available. With so many choices, it is imperative that you seek professional advice. There are pluses and minuses to the newer more creative loans so read all the fine print before making any financing decisions. If you are already a homeowner, your current lender may be a good source for a new mortgage. Your realtor can also refer you to mortgage brokers with whom they have successfully worked.

The internet and business section of the newspaper provides the most up to date rates from leading lenders for you to compare. The bank where you have accounts and an established relationship can assist you too. Your bank wants your business and loyalty, so they should be happy to help you and will probably offer you a better interest rate than an unfamiliar customer.

In summation, do your homework! As an experienced educator and mother, I feel very comfortable making that necessary statement. Review your credit report, get out your calculator to learn what you can comfortably afford, and gather as much home lending information as you can. If you choose to buy your next home, it is to your advantage to spend ample time "shopping around" for the best mortgage rate and plan available to you. As soon as you thoroughly complete this step, get a letter of qualification from the lender and you will be ready to proceed to the next chapter.

Chapter Eight Check List

- Find out your credit score and get reports from all three major credit bureaus.

- Inform the bureaus of all errors you discover in your reports immediately.

- Pay off debt if it will improve your credit worthiness.

- Decide what monthly loan or rental payment you are willing and capable of paying.

- Use the basic affordability formulas to calculate the amount you can pay.

- Determine how much money you have for a down payment.

- Budget enough money to pay your estimated closing costs.

- Shop around for the best mortgage rates and plans to suite your needs.

- Review the free booklets available from Fannie Mae if you desire further information.

- Obtain a letter of qualification from your intended lender.

9 | Shopping for Your New Home

After carefully considering the financial points made in the previous chapter, you have now determined how much you can and want to spend on your new home. If you are already a homeowner, I strongly suggest you have a contract of impending sale on your current residence prior to beginning serious house hunting. You might think about putting the sale of your home as a contingency clause on the purchase agreement for your new home. The seller may or may not want to take an offer with this type of contingency and offer you the "right of first refusal". Since you are unsure about how long your home may be in the marketing phase, you don't want to rush to go to contract with a new house and possibly end up having to pay two mortgages simultaneously. You also don't want to find a dream house and suffer disappointment if the timing of a closing does not truly fit your needs and pocketbook.

If you have carefully evaluated your situation and you are feeling comfortable, it is time to commence your housing search. Begin by obtaining a detailed map of the location in which you are interested. Pinpoint the site(s) of employment and places you would travel to on a frequent basis such as schools and shopping centers. Draw a circle enclosing the areas within a reasonable commuting distance. Keep in mind that a seemingly short distance can mean an hour commute in areas with heavy traffic! Some people are comfortable with an hour or more commuting time while others feel the need to live almost next door to their place of employment. Other possible considerations include the availability of mass transit to and from the workplace. If you have the option of taking a train, subway or bus to your job, you may be willing to live a bit further away since someone else will be doing the driving for you. Using public transit can make the commute less stressful and costly. Long commutes result in tremendous wear and tear on a vehicle and are draining on the mind and body. My husband and I have experienced commutes as long as ninety minutes and as short as ten minutes. Without a doubt, the shorter the travel time, the easier life is for the whole family.

It is critical that you consider neighborhood desirability when making your housing selection. At one time my husband worked in an area zoned for factories and warehouses. We decided to live in a housing development about forty five minutes away from his office because we could not find or afford a safer family friendly environment nearby. As concerned parents, we were willing to make a commuting sacrifice in exchange for a higher quality of life for our daughters. I know of other individuals who have been fortunate enough to find suitable housing within walking distance of their jobs. Take ample time to decide what commute and lifestyle is most agreeable with your situation before zeroing in on your targeted search region. I strongly urge you to experience the commute to work during rush hour prior to making your final housing decision.

Now that you have drawn the circle on your map, begin your search. Real estate websites, local newspapers and real estate agents are probably your best initial sources for finding property listings and available rentals. Information about financing a home, moving companies, as well as household and gardening tips can be found on www.realtor.com. Probably the most helpful aspect of this website is the ability to view real estate from all fifty states in every price range from your computer at your convenience. Type in the city, state or zip code you are interested in moving to, the number of bedrooms and bathrooms you desire and the appropriate price range for your budget. In just moments, much of the available housing in that area will appear at your fingertips.

You can then narrow your search by clicking on "more search options" and you can specify certain features you require or value in a home. You can select property type such as single family, condominium, mobile home or rental property. You can choose features such as minimum square footage, age of home, garage, laundry, basement, den and even disability accommodations. Lot preferences such as waterfront, mountain views, city views or corner parcels can be indicated too. You can even specify whether you prefer a community which provides a club house, exercise facilities, golf course, security gates, tennis courts, pool and other recreational choices. I suggest you examine all the search options to help you decide what kind of housing is most appealing to you. For example, you may desire three bedrooms, two bathrooms, an attached garage, fireplace, central air conditioning, a basement and hardwood floors. You might want an older home on an acre lot with a pool, or perhaps you are only interested in a newly constructed high rise condominium with an ocean view. Whatever your preferences, you can indicate your search criteria on www.realtor.com and then this website can provide property listings that most closely match your particular housing requirements and wishes. I must point out that while most of us want to live in our dream home, the majority of us still have a budget to think about and flexibility with our housing desires may be necessary.

Almost every internet listed property, especially single family homes, shows a front photograph of the house along with an identification number or MLS (multiple listing) number, listing price, the name of the real estate agent and agency holding the listing and a general description. If you click to request more information, you can usually check out the estimated monthly payment or PITI (the acronym used for principal, interest, taxes and insurance based on a 20% down payment and a traditional thirty year fixed current rate mortgage), square footage, year built, and style or design of the house such as contemporary or traditional. You can often find number of rooms, room dimensions, appliance and utilities information such as whether the house has sewer or septic service, and whether it is heated with gas, electricity or oil. Building materials used for exterior walls, roofing and even interior flooring may be indicated here. Architectural features like front porches and any extra amenities which include central vacuum systems, spas and bidets will usually be mentioned amongst the details. Some internet listings are very comprehensive while others are much less descriptive.

In addition, I want to point out that annual property taxes, any applicable neighborhood association fees and the school assignment information are almost always displayed with each marketed home. The taxes, fees and assigned schools are very crucial components of your housing decisions. Your budget must allow for housing expenses above and beyond the basic mortgage payment, and the quality of the schools plays a large part in calculating the overall value of your new home. I will discuss educational considerations in greater detail later in this chapter.

It is sometimes possible to view the actual interior and

immediate exterior of a house through posted photographs or even a virtual tour. If a listing provides these enhancements, you can download these visual aids. Sit back, relax and tour the property without leaving your chair! This amazing technology enables you to quickly retain or dismiss a listing thus saving you lots of time and effort. Take full advantage!

Hopefully, you will find some properties that interest you or at least you gather some useful information that will help you as you continue hunting. If you see some homes that you like, note the MLS #s for identification purposes so you can easily find them the next time you search the web. You can also click on the "save this listing" spot on the website to quickly review the listings later. If you are really intrigued by a listing, contact the realtor or realty company that is presenting the property. You can email or phone them directly requesting further information. You can even schedule an actual showing of the property via email. They will be very happy to hear from you and eager to assist you with your search because they love to serve serious buyers! Remember they don't receive their commission checks without facilitating an actual sale. If they are not extremely responsive and helpful, it is best to find someone else who will serve you more effectively and efficiently. Any realtor can show you a property as long as he or she is licensed in the intended area.

As I mentioned in an earlier chapter, if you hired a real estate agent to sell your current home, he or she can assist you in your search of another home if you are making a local move. If you are relocating to an area outside of the region, the realtor can put you in touch with another qualified realtor in your new location. They are thrilled to do this because they earn a finder's fee if you actually employ the services of the recommended agent. Just be certain that the suggested agent is someone you are comfortable dealing with before engaging in a working relationship. Unfortunately some realtors deserve the "pushy" reputation sometimes found in that profession. Patience on their part is essential when you are carefully weighing your options as you hunt for what is usually your greatest asset and expense.

If you are moving to a large metropolitan area such as New York City or Chicago, you will quickly discover that there are a myriad of options in the surrounding areas and neighbor-hoods. In this case, you are likely to require the expertise of more than one realtor because they generally are licensed and familiar within specific vicinities. When my husband's career required us to move to the New York City region, we worked with agents in New York, New Jersey and even Connecticut before making our housing selection. Reliable public transportation enables many who work in the city to explore a wider territory. Whatever your requirements, you can find the help you need through email, your current realtor, and possibly even a friend or relative who resides or has lived in the intended area. In fact, a trusted and knowl-edgeable person(s) who will receive no financial gain from your relocation is likely to be your best source of information since they want to see you as happily settled as possible and will remain in your life long after the realtors finish their services. Listen care-fully to the advice of those who know you and the area well.

Once you have made the appropriate contacts and have accu-mulated as much information as possible, begin to evaluate your findings. With advanced research, it is relatively easy to narrow in on the options that intrigue you the most. I was able to limit my serious house hunting to a few neighborhoods every time we relocated by carefully investigating the characteristics of each town in my home search region. Crime statistics, school reports, population density, cultural offerings, cost of living and proxim-ity to conveniences are important aspects of every community which require thorough investigation before making any decision to settle anywhere. Real estate agents and investors often say "location, location, location" when determining the value and degree of desirability of a property. There is much truth to this statement, but choose your home based on your priorities and the factors that are most suitable for you.

As a mother, experienced educator and transient American who has also had vast house hunting adventures, I feel I must discuss school reports separately and in greater detail than some of the other considerations when evaluating an area. I have learned the availability of a quality education is highly significant to most people when purchasing or renting a home whether they have school aged children or not. Good schools always have a positive impact on a community, not only because they increase property values by drawing more buyers, but especially because crime rates generally decline where schools are strong. Excellent school systems encourage the development of quality students and in turn build quality communities. In other words, successful neighborhoods usually support successful schools and successful schools build solid neighborhoods. Even if you have no children, a local educational system will impact your life. You may have children in the future who will attend the schools; if you buy a home, you will be obligated to pay a substantial percentage of your property tax to support the assigned schools and even continually hear about the schools through the daily media. It is best to carefully study the school reports before making any housing decision.

Every realtor and school system should provide you with the most up to date school reports upon request. This is public information and should be readily available. www.Schoolmatch. com can also help you find appropriate school information. If you have difficulty following the results, almost any educator can help you interpret the statistics. Some items to help you determine school quality are class sizes, percentage of high school students who actually earn diplomas, percentage of high school graduates who attend college, where they attend college, money spent per pupil, availability of extra curricular programs, teacher credentials, standardized test score results for every grade tested, and average scores of college entrance examinations.

In general, you want small class sizes or low teacher-student ratios. Teachers can focus more on individual students when he or she is responsible for fewer children. School systems which have students matriculating to nationally recognized colleges usually have an excellent college preparatory curriculum in place. If the community truly values education, the citizens are usually willing to pay for it, resulting in higher per pupil spending than the national average. School systems which require teacher certification and continuing teacher education often have highly qualified faculties. If schools offer a variety of extracurricular activities, they indicate a concern for the pupils in all areas of their lives. Access to athletics, special interest clubs, performing arts, and quality after school care all keep children occupied with worthwhile activities which broaden their perspectives, improve their life skills and keep them safe and out of trouble.

In addition, careful review of recent test results often indicates a school's degree of success. Each area of the country selects standardized tests for the lower grades that they feel are most appropriate to measure the skills of their students. Some states, such as Florida and California have developed their own tests. Some more commonly used tests are the Iowa Tests and the Stanford Achievement Tests. Tests called Regents' Exams are utilized in some areas too. Colleges and universities require applicants to submit scores from the American College Test (ACT) and/or the Scholastic Aptitude Test (SAT). Every school system whether public, private or parochial, should provide recent statistics when requested to help you discover where their students stand compared to the national averages. The higher the scores, the more likely the schools have met the needs of the students and the demands of society.

Sometimes it is necessary to move to a location where the schools are less than stellar. Let's face it, some states and regions have weaker schools than others. In this event, there are often an abundance of private school options. You may have a special needs child to accommodate who requires you to further research the learning institutions in the intended area. We have had our children in outstanding public schools in some locations and enrolled them in private schools when we felt it necessary in other areas. I recommend visiting schools while they are in session to get an even better perspective before deciding on any community. If you are moving with children, bring them along, review information together and encourage them to share their feelings. By the time our daughters reached the age of ten, their opinions strongly influenced all our school and neighborhood choices. Remember the school your child attends has an even bigger impact on them than you, so involve them as much as possible. I advise you to treat the school investigation portion of your house hunting as a matter of paramount importance.

Hopefully, after some very careful research, you have been able to narrow your housing hunt. Contact the listing agents of several homes that appear suitable for your needs. Make appointments to view the available homes as soon as possible, since they may become unavailable in the near future. Remember other potential buyers may be interested in them too. Always attempt to be as prompt and courteous to the seller as possible. If you have recently marketed your home, you are aware of how it feels to have your home examined and invaded by strangers. When you go to see the properties, be sure to take a pad of paper and pencil to makes notes about the homes' details and jot down questions you may want to ask later. This is especially important if you will be visiting more than one home each day. I often got features of the homes confused when I saw several properties in one day. My notes helped me recall one listing from another. Drawing a simple floor plan might jog your memory too.

Sometimes you can dismiss a property the minute you see the surrounding neighborhood. For example, you may desire a quiet street and a property is situated across from a busy supermarket or school yard. Other times you are delighted by the curb appeal of a house, but are disappointed with the interior floor plan and maintenance. If this happens, it is best to politely thank the realtor and to honestly express your opinions. Remember you are on an important mission and want to use your time wisely. The real estate agent assisting you is also interested in efficiency. The more you communicate, the better he or she will understand your requirements.

It is important to keep an open mind when you are shopping for your new home. No home is perfect. Even if you decide that no existing house will suit you, buying new construction is far from ideal too. Building a home takes an enormous amount of time and energy and usually requires almost endless patience. Builders rarely deliver a completed home on schedule due to weather constraints, material backorders, workers scheduling problems, etc. They often make numerous mistakes too, so you have to have the time and ability to closely keep an eye on the entire building project. You should be available to point out errors and omissions on an almost daily basis. These delays can add up to many months and force you into paying for a temporary rental, additional moving expenses and unwanted storage fees. Adding a second move into your relocation process is only going to further complicate your life. My husband and I contracted to build houses from the ground up twice. Yes, it was fun and exciting to select a floor plan, fixtures, flooring, cabinetry, countertops and paint colors, but neither construction project went as smoothly as we had expected. We experienced plenty of glitches and headaches along the way. Building is not the glamorous route that it seems. Trust me on this one. I could write another book on this subject! By all means, build your own house if you cannot find any existing home that satisfies you. Eventually, you will get settled, but prepare yourself for a potentially much longer transitional period.

If you decide to undertake the building experience, I strongly suggest you do your best to learn about a builder before signing a construction contract. If you are considering building in a new development, talk to the neighbors who have recently moved in. Were they satisfied with the builder? Why or why not? Would they recommend the builder and has warranty work been handled effectively and efficiently? Most new construction is completely guaranteed for a full calendar year. Appliances usually are covered by the manufacturers and items like roofing and plumbing often carry much longer warranties. Check out the builder's reputation by contacting the Better Business Bureau. J.D. Powers and Associates also may have conducted a survey on the building company. Obtain copies of any available reports to discover the builder's and developer's reputations before signing a binding contract with any construction company.

Builders' prices reflect a long list of specific materials. Carefully review the level of quality and what items are considered standard or included in the price and what items are upgrades or extras. Chances are you will decide to make some changes to the plans, upgrade some finishes or chose to even customize to your taste. Be aware that any changes from the developer's original plans add to your overall costs. It is best to make most of your selections before signing a contract to get the real price before building commences. If you do not have everything in writing from the beginning, you may end up paying much more in the end than you want or can afford. Any alterations, even changing a paint color can result in additional fees. Adding a soap ledge to the master bath shower in one of my newly built homes resulted in a work order charge of $250! As ridiculous as that seems, some builders really make their profits through work order changes and luxury details. Proceed with great caution.

If you find an existing home that fulfills almost all of your requirements and desires, but has decorations that makes you squint, remember that can easily be changed. You can remove visually disturbing wall coverings and ghastly draperies the second you own it! A fresh coat of paint in your favorite color can be applied quickly too. On the other hand, if the house cries out for a new kitchen, completely updated bathrooms or any other major remodeling, it may be best to continue looking for another house. However, if you have the resources, and the endurance to take on major home projects, you may relish the thoughts of a "fixer upper" or "handyman's special." It is your choice.

Once in a while a house "feels right" the minute you walk into the foyer. Emotions can come into play very easily here, so be careful. Remember the old saying "buyer beware." I suggest you thoroughly investigate the property you are "falling in love with." Closely examine each room taking notes as you go through the home. You should visit the house two or three times because it is difficult to see everything clearly in just one viewing. Drawing a simple sketch of the floor plan can help you visualize things too. Be sure to look in all the closets, the garage and the basement. Take a stroll around the perimeter of the house to get completely familiar with the yard and the exterior of the house itself. Take the time to closely evaluate the landscaping and general condition of any outside features such as air conditioning units, gutters, walls, windows, patios, decks, and sidewalks. Make yourself aware of the traffic patterns and noise near the house. Unless you plan to live in an urban area, traffic sounds can be very distracting. What areas of the house get morning and afternoon sun? Afternoon sun streaming into the kitchen and family room area where people spend most of their time can be delightful in a cool climate and miserable in a warmer climate. Note plenty of details and any concerns.

If you still feel good about the property, it is time to thoroughly evaluate the neighborhood. If you love the house, but don't like the neighborhood, you will not be happy living there. Spend time in the neighborhood. Do most residents take appropriate care of their property? Does the surrounding area provide the amenities you desire such as diverse shopping, ample restaurant selections, easy access to transportation or roadways, a local library, places of worship, low crime rates, good schools, cultural opportunities, and recreational options such as parks and theaters? Take the time to stroll around the area and chat with neighbors and shopkeepers. Check out the grocery store and nearby restaurants. Visit a school and even a playground. Stop by the town hall and ask the receptionist about recent local happenings and events. The police station is another worthwhile place to visit so you can ask about crime statistics. Do not be shy. Talk to many residents and get as complete a picture of your potential residence as possible. Keep in mind you are about to make the biggest investment of your life. Your home and neighborhood play a huge role in your daily existence. Therefore, educating yourself before deciding to purchase any home is time well spent. If you look at all this as an adventure, you will actually enjoy this part of the moving process.

- Have a contract of impending sale on your current property.

- Purchase a detailed map of your intended location.

- Pinpoint the sites of importance such as workplace(s), schools, and amenities.

- Investigate commuting options. Consider driving congestion and mass transit.

- Encircle important sites within a reasonable commuting distance.

- Gather local newspapers and real estate publications to begin your house hunting.

- Search the real estate websites for property listings and available rentals.

- Remember to remain flexible with your choices if you have budget restrictions.

- Keep the property taxes and possible association fees in mind when calculating costs.

- Note the MLS #s and contact information of the housing options that interest you.

- Contact the listing agent of the intriguing properties to request more information.

- Allow yourself extra search time if you are moving to a large metropolitan area.

- Obtain the area crime and population statistics, cultural offerings and amenities.

- Study the area school reports and follow the suggestions given in this book.

- Investigate the availability of private education if applicable to your situation.

- Visit area schools to help you further narrow your search.

- Contact the listing agents to schedule meetings and view properties.

- Take detailed notes while viewing each property to avoid future confusion.

- Sketch a simple floor plan of each house to help you recall it later.

- Eliminate any housing that does not meet your requirements, but keep an open mind.

- Consider new construction if you cannot find appropriate existing housing.

- Decide to build a new home only after carefully considering the pros and cons.

- Visit the preferable properties once or twice more. Examine every inch of the houses.

- Check out the neighborhood surroundings and talk to people who live there.

- Commute to your place of employment to evaluate your daily travel experience.

- Rank the homes in order of preference and phone the agents with your decisions.

10 | Making an Offer

You have now completed your search and have found the home of your dreams! Perhaps it is not the castle you will buy when you win the lottery, but it fits your needs and makes you and your family happy! Sit down with your realtor, review every detail on the buyer's disclosure forms and inquire about any possible concerns. If the seller's remarks and answers are acceptable to you, it is time to prepare an agreement of sale. Recognize that the price you offer to pay the seller for the home is probably the most important term in the contract, but the non-monetary terms are also very important. The purchase agreement should explain in detail what guarantees exist, what the closing costs will be and what recourse both parties have if the contract is not fulfilled. Carefully consider the price you want to offer and the terms you desire. You will request a specific date of closing, reveal your financing plans, request a home inspection, pest inspection, and list any items you may want included in the purchase that have not been mentioned in the MLS listing. Some items buyers frequently ask for are washers and dryers, window treatments, and custom built furnishings. If you want some additional items, be prepared to raise your offer. Also, have a valid check ready that will serve as your earnest payment. This payment is usually at least $1000. If the offer is accepted you will then have to make an additional agreed upon deposit within a specified number of days. Your money will lock in the right to purchase the home once the terms are agreed upon between you and the seller.

Your real estate agent will provide a contract that is usually the standard form used in the region or state in which he or she works. You may make changes or additions to the agreement, but remember the seller must agree to every alteration you make. If you are a first time buyer, it is wise to hire an attorney to review the contract to tell you if it protects your interests in the event the deal fails to materialize. A simple addendum or change in the text can make the contract more suitable for your needs. Your realtor can usually recommend a competent attorney. Before hiring an attorney, be sure to inquire about what services will be performed and for what fee. Ask about his or her experience and whether he/she will be involved through settlement or closing. In some locations attorneys act as settlement/closing agents or as escrow agents to handle settlements. An attorney who performs all these services may also represent the interests of the seller and the lender, so be sure you feel comfortable with the attorney selected. In many parts of the country, attorneys are not involved in transfers of real estate. In California, for example, escrow agents or escrow companies handle all the paperwork to transfer titles without any attorney involvement. In this case, I still suggest a legal review of a sales contract to anyone unfamiliar with real estate transactions. Expert advice can explain and simplify the process for the novice. The legal fees you pay are well worth it if they protect you from incurring costs and hardship down the road.

Carefully consider the amount you offer before writing the

contract. If you really like the property, it is best to be fair with the price. We have had some potential buyers make insultingly low offers that accomplished nothing but created ill feelings. In all cases, these individuals were turned away and our houses were later sold to other people. Do not begin the negotiating process by aggravating the homeowner. Generally speaking, I would advise against making any offer that is less than 90% of the asking price. Check out comparable listings and recent sales to determine if the price seems reasonable, low or elevated. Also, find out how long the property has been on the market and how eager the owners are to sell. You can learn through public records what the owner paid when he purchased the property. Remember, he hopes to make some profit just like you do on your sale. Your real estate agent can easily access this data for you by doing a CMA or Competitive Marketing Analysis. All this information can help you decide on a reasonable amount to offer.

Think about when you want to move in and select a closing date. You should try to close on your previous property first so you have your funds from that house accessible for expenses associated with the new one. Your lending agent can probably provide a "bridge loan" if necessary in the event you experience any transaction delays. This is a common problem that can usually be handled easily, especially if the funds are only needed for a short time. It is also important to consider other scheduled dates before choosing one for closing. When will a new job start? When do you want your children to transition to a new school? Should they finish the current term or should they finish the ongoing school year where they are now enrolled? Perhaps you want to take possession of the new house prior to leaving the old one to allow you to complete a decorating or remodeling project before moving in. Evaluate your circumstances and desires before selecting a settlement date.

The house may contain items that you would like included in the sale that may or may not have been mentioned in the MLS listing. Maybe you love the porch furniture which coordinates perfectly with the attached awning. You might really like to have the bedspread in the guestroom which matches the custom made draperies. Sometimes an item such as a customized cabinet that has been made especially for a particular space can be difficult to duplicate. In these cases, it is a good idea to include specific extras in the contract. We have frequently relinquished electronics, bar stools, exterior planted pots, rugs that match décor and large appliances. Understand that the seller may have emotional attachments to some belongings, so do not lose a great house over possessions, but do include them in your offer if you really want the things. The seller may even be relieved to not have to move these items. We bought a house from sellers who were downsizing after their children had grown. They were very happy to not have to worry about what to do with their excess furnishings.

The contract will indicate whether or not you want a home inspection. I believe this is essential even though you as the buyer usually pay for this service. The report may prevent you from getting stuck with an inferior house which will become a major headache and revenue drain. Insist on a complete structural inspection and pest inspection. Environmental inspections are also crucial if applicable to the location. For example a water quality evaluation is required if the home has a septic system, radon levels may need to be monitored for air safety in some regions, and lead based paint and asbestos risks may also need to be revealed if the home was built prior to 1978. If hazards are discovered or expensive repairs need to be made, you may cancel the agreement, or require the seller to make all the repairs and eradicate any environmental problems to your satisfaction prior to closing. All repairs must be done in a timely manner at the seller's expense.

The mortgage clause will indicate how you plan to pay for the property. All the specifics about the type of financing you plan to have in place are detailed here. You will need to inform the seller of how much you plan to put down on the property and how much you will be financing. If you are putting down less than 20%, you may be required to purchase mortgage insurance. Will you be using a conventional, adjustable rate, Federal Housing Administration (FHA), Veterans' Administration (VA), or other type of loan? The interest rate and other fees and points you will pay are also noted in this clause. A point is usually equal to one percent of the loan amount and is paid to the lender at closing to obtain a lower interest rate. Hopefully, you will have heeded my advice from an earlier chapter and have a letter or mortgage approval already in hand by the time you write an offer. Sellers are much more eager to do business with a well qualified purchaser.

The contract will often request the homeowner to provide a professional land survey indicating property lines, deed and evidence of title to the property. The title refers to the legal ownership of the home. The title should be free and clear of all claims to the property. Any claims to the property are called encumbrances or liens. If any problems exist, the purchaser may cancel the contract or allow the seller to attempt to repair the defects. If the troubles are adequately remedied, the seller should obtain title insurance to protect the purchaser in the event trouble resurfaces. The title search and title insurance are typically paid by the seller. The survey can be paid by either party and might be negotiable.

Other paragraphs on closing credits, costs and adjustments may be included in the agreement. Real estate broker commissions, utilities adjustments, prorated utility costs, assessments and other costs specific to the property may be noted. Cancellation procedures will be addressed as will handling of escrow monies, continued property maintenance on the part of the seller until closing, and other miscellaneous details may be included in the contract as required by the locality and involved parties.

You should make your offer in writing since a verbal offer is not binding. Your real estate agent will contact the homeowner to arrange a meeting to present your offer as soon as possible. It is best to request a response to your offer within a set number of business days so that all parties are communicating in a timely and respectful manner. It is unusual for there to be no negotiations. Hopefully they are just minor adjustments and all goes swiftly and smoothly. If you write a reasonable and fair offer, you should be able to come to terms with each other quickly and then celebrate as you look forward to a new life in your next home.

Chapter Ten Check List

- Meet with the realtor to review the buyer's disclosures and inquire about any concerns.

- Find out how long the house has been on the market and what the sellers paid for it.

- Check out the recent sales in the area of comparable homes.

- Review all your findings and determine the price you will offer to pay for the property.

- Select a closing date convenient for you.

- Decide if there are any additional items you would like included in the sale.

- Indicate that you would like to have the house thoroughly inspected.

- Provide the details concerning your financing plans.

- Prepare the agreement of sale documents with the real estate agent or an attorney.

- Hire an attorney to review all documents, especially if you are a new buyer or leaser.

11 | Choosing a Moving Company

You now know where you, your family and your belongings will be headed, but how will everyone and everything travel from point A to point B? The time has come to plan for the physical part of the move. Hopefully, you have already heeded my earlier advice and have purged and donated all unwanted and unnecessary items. Careful evaluation of your next residence will probably enable you to eliminate even more stuff. The new kitchen might have a trash compactor allowing you to trash your trash container. Maybe you can get rid of your standing bookcases because the new place has built-in shelving. Continually keep in mind that moving costs are based mostly on weight, so the more you move, the more it will cost. Even if you are fortunate enough to have your employer pay for most of your move, you still want to keep expenditures down since many employers now provide a lump sum or set a ceiling for your relocation costs. Moving almost always costs more than you initially anticipate, so try to be as economical as possible with the things you can control since you may have to make some adjustments with your planning and budget.

Begin to assess your particular situation. If you are moving from an apartment or small house with only a few rooms of furniture, you might want to rent a truck, pack yourself, and secure the helping hands of several strong bodied friends. This is probably the preferable method if you are moving locally. Be sure to compare rates of the do-it-yourself companies located near you such as Ryder and U-Haul. Check out The Yellow Pages and internet for locations, availability and rates. Rental trucks and vans are in greater demand on weekends, so plan ahead and book early if you require weekend usage. Be aware that advertisements may state a daily fee, but that is often misleading. Most will charge a mileage rate, higher weekend rates, a supply fee if you desire a dolly or ramp to ease the loading, a fuel replenishing charge, and possibly a late fee if you keep the vehicle any longer than the reserved time. Look at the fine print for any tardiness penalties. These truck lenders may also ask you to purchase insurance. If you have insurance on your own vehicle and use a credit card to pay for the rental, you are probably already protected. Check with your insurer and credit card issuer before paying for any unnecessary coverage. Be aware that they often try to pressure you to buy insurance. Do not fall prey to this sales pitch if you do not need it. If you are moving outside of your area, you will be charged an extra fee to drop the rental vehicle off at a location that differs from the point of origin.

An option you may want to investigate is PODS (the acronym for personal on demand storage). Information about this alternative type of moving and storage can be found at www.pods.com. I have no experience with this relatively new company, but have seen it advertised frequently in recent months. Their website states they provide storage containers, warehouses and transport systems to new locations. It may well be worth your time to check out PODS.

If you are moving within the same general area, you might want to consider using a local moving company instead of loading, unloading and driving yourself. Local moves are usually based on an hourly rate instead of weight. Compare the total costs before signing anything. I have assisted my daughter with several moves within the same area and have learned that the $19.95 rates painted on the sides of the trucks usually end up in the $250.00 range once all the fees and taxes are calculated. Once, after packing all the boxes ourselves, we paid a local company an hourly rate to move four rooms of furniture to another home several miles from the first home. The total bill was approximately $350.00. We were also able to buy damage insurance through them so that if any of the large furnishings broke while they were handling it, we could recoup repair or replacement costs. Of course, they did all the back breaking work quickly and much more efficiently than we could have. In our case, the moving company was well worth the extra dollars we spent.

If you are relocating to a new area and have more than a few rooms of furnishings, I advise you to hire a professional moving company. Begin by asking friends, neighbors and family members for recommendations. They are usually eager to tell their horror stories of escalating costs, poor service and lost and damaged goods. Heed their warnings and follow their recommendations. Once you have a list, check out the Better Business Bureau at www.bbb.org and the Public Service Commission at www.psc.us under the transportation section. Both sites provide report cards and complaints lodged against companies. There is no need to contact a company if these sites display poor evaluations. You may also want to check out www.movingscam.com and www. moving.org for additional hints on finding reliable movers, getting estimates, filing complaints and planning for moving day.

Narrow your list to three moving companies and schedule

appointments with each one to have their representatives come to your home for an on-site consultation. Go through every inch of your home with them. They will inspect every cupboard, closet and space in your home to provide an estimated moving cost. If you are leaving any items behind such as appliances, it is best to clearly mark them before they arrive so there is no confusion and your estimate can be as accurate as possible. Let them know specifically when you need to move and when you would like to arrive at your new location. If you want to have the movers do the packing, you must allow time for that to be completed when you plan your schedule. You may have to be flexible by a day or two especially if you want to move during the summer months when movers are busiest. Also the middle of the month is usually an easier time to reserve the movers because many leases expire the first or last part of the month making the demand for movers' services less during the second or third weeks.

Trust me when I say that you should insist on a written, not-to-exceed, binding estimate which includes specific loading and unloading dates. Movers will provide written estimates, but you want to be certain that you obtain a binding estimate because estimates without guarantees are often inaccurate and the real charges may be higher. Years ago while moving from Washington D.C. to Florida my sister signed a non-binding moving contract. She got a call the night before the delivery and was told she had to present a cashier's check the following morning that was several hundred dollars more than the original estimate or they would not unload her belongings. It was like they were holding her furniture hostage. She had no choice but to pay the inflated bill. Unfortunately, that mover took advantage of her youth and inexperience. There are enough potential headaches during times of transition without having to worry about growing expenses and unpleasant surprises. In addition, have whomever you hire agree in writing to reimburse you for any costs you incur if they cannot pick up or deliver on the promised dates.

Know ahead of time whether you plan to drive to your new location or if you need to have your vehicle(s) transported by a car carrier. The company may have a service that can help you with that portion of the move too. I have utilized the services of a car carrier company twice and suggest you pay extra to top load your vehicle to avoid fluid spillage during transport coming from cars loaded above yours. Believe me if you are concerned about your car's finish, you will not want skimp and bottom load your wheels. The rates for automobile transport are based mostly on distance. If you are relocated within a day's drive, it is probably much more economical to drive yourself. If you are moving across country, you might want to seriously consider hiring a car carrier because it takes several days to travel across the United States. The gasoline is expensive, the added mileage on your vehicle depreciates its value and paying for lodging along the way can get costly. If you choose to drive, you can load your car up with the items you will need and want to keep with you such as clothing, toiletries, important files, medications, photo albums and of course, the kids, Spot or Fluffy and your houseplants.

Sometimes due to timing glitches it becomes necessary to store your things instead of moving them directly from one location to another. Perhaps you've sold your home and are unable to close on the new one as soon as you would ideally want. Maybe your lease is expiring and you have still not found the right home. Whatever the situation, if you need to store your belongings, let the moving companies you interview know this upfront. I think it is best to have the same people handle your belongings from beginning to end. Most large movers have their own storage facilities where they crate your load and keep it locked up until you are ready for delivery. We have done this several times and have not had any problems. I chose to store at the point of origination because I was able to inspect the facility and familiarize myself with the staff there before finally selecting a moving company. It was easy to work with people and a facility where I already felt comfortable. Remember the movers are responsible for the safekeeping of your load from the time they take possession of it until they deliver it to your new home. This includes storage time.

It is also crucial to familiarize yourself with your current insurance coverage prior to the moving companies' visits. Some home owner's policies will insure your belongings throughout the move providing you will be insuring with them in your new home too. You may not need to buy full coverage from the movers if you are adequately covered through your current policy. I have always had the benefit of continuous coverage with my home owner's policy, but have decided to purchase the insurance through the moving company as well. I felt more comfortable having an extra "safety net" in the event I had severe damage and had trouble collecting from one or the other.

Movers usually offer two types of insurance. Basic coverage is called released value coverage and claims are settled based on the weight of damaged, lost or destroyed items. Sixty cents per pound is a typical liability rate. In other words, a ten pound computer might cost $1,000.00 to replace, but if that same laptop is destroyed during a move, you would only get $.60 x 10 lbs. or $6.00 for it. This is because basic coverage reimburses losses based on weight alone. Most movers do not charge for this minimal protection. The old saying "you get what you pay for" holds true here. Do not even consider agreeing to this type of insurance, because I guarantee that there will be some damage following the transport of your goods. I have never been without a few dents or scratches that required me to file a claim. I urge you to select what is called full value coverage. This option requires the mover to satisfactorily repair, replace or settle with cash the full replacement value of any lost or damaged article(s). Typically, the minimum declared value for this type of insurance is $5,000.00. You may elect to reduce the cost of coverage by agreeing to a $250 or $500 deductible. I would discourage you from choosing to take a deductible since mover's liability insurance is relatively inexpensive and the deductible may cause some difficulties when handling claims. For example, full value protection is roughly $8.50 for each $1,000.00 of declared value. This translates to $170.00 for $20,000 of declared value. Simplify things and protect yourself by agreeing to purchase full value coverage with no deductible. That way you will avoid trouble handling minor damage claims.

Have your home tidy and in order before each mover's agent arrives. He or she will carefully examine the contents of your home to determine the weight of your shipment and what types of containers you need. They are amazingly well trained to make an accurate estimate. Be prepared to discuss any additional services you may want them to provide. Do you want them to give you a quote for packing the entire house or just some selected items? You might consider getting quotes for packing everything, for packing some things, and for doing all the packing yourself. If you pack yourself, do you want them to provide boxes, wrapping paper and tape? Do they have gently used boxes available that you can purchase at a reduced price? Do you have certain items that you wish them to pack in crates or disassemble and reassemble? Be sure to point out items of extraordinary value that may require extra care or a bit more insurance. Extraordinary value is generally an item with a value exceeding $100 per pound. Artwork or autographed sports memorabilia might qualify as objects of extraordinary value that you should itemize in your inventory for special attention. We have a grand-father clock that has always required special packaging and set up. The associated fees should be part of your entire binding estimate. Pianos, especially baby grand styles need special pack-ing to ensure safe, damage free delivery. If you want cartons for mattresses and bed set up, you need to specify those services at the time of the visit too.

If your budget is not too tight, I would strongly encourage you to have the movers do the packing. Not only will it save you time and labor, but movers are only responsible for dam-age to the cartons they have packed. They are always liable for large furnishings that they wrap and put on the truck, but since they have no idea how carefully you packed a box, they are not responsible if your china is broken en route to your new address. I have learned the hard way that movers are not as careful while loading the truck when you have packed things yourself. Cartons are typically just stacked on top of each other without regard to contents. If you pack yourself, clearly mark everything in bold letters so that heavy pots are not placed on top of lampshades and your books are not set on top of your glassware. If you truly value your things and can afford it, pay the movers to do the packing. This especially applies to breakables such as china, crys-tal and glassware.

As soon as you have your three binding estimates, it is time to carefully review each one to determine which mover to hire. You may want to visit the companies' facilities especially if you require storage. Are the sites clean and the employees welcom-ing, helpful and pleasant? If you do not feel comfortable, cross that company off your list. You may want to consider a well known company because they often have offices all over the country to assist you. A larger firm will have a fleet that trans-ports worldwide everyday, enabling them to guarantee pick up and delivery dates that are convenient for you. Be careful, if you chose a nationally known company, that they can still provide the personal customer service that you deserve. Also the lowest price is not always the way to go. Do business with whichever company you feel will provide you with the most complete and caring service possible. Transitions are difficult enough without having to worry about the many details that the moving company is paid to perform.

- Review the features of your future home and eliminate any unsuitable belongings.

- Assess the possible ways to move the contents of your current home to your new one.

- Elect to do it yourself, use a local mover, or hire a professional moving company.

- Research the rates and available dates of rental trucks if you chose to do it yourself.

- Compare the cost of self moving with those of hiring movers to determine best value.

- Ask your friends, neighbors and relatives for moving company recommendations.

- Investigate each recommended moving company using the websites noted in this book.

- Narrow your list to two or three reputable companies and schedule appointments.

- Mark all items you plan to leave behind so your estimate is as accurate as possible.

- Know when you want to move out and when you want to move in your new place.

- Think about whether you or the movers will do the packing.

- Give each moving company representative a complete tour of your home.

- Discuss insurance options with the representatives and select the best choice for you.

- Decide how you plan to move your vehicle(s). The movers may offer this service.

- Ask the representatives about temporary storage if you have a timing concern.

- Notify the movers of items that require special packing such as pianos and artwork.

- Review all estimates and select the company you believe will provide the best service.

12 | Attention to Details

All your big decisions have been made. You now know where you are moving, when you are moving, what your new home is like, and how you are getting everything and everyone there. If time allows, take a couple days off to recharge yourself. Relax with a good book, go to lunch with a friend, get a massage, do whatever you like to reward yourself for getting this far. You surely deserve it.

After a bit of a break, it is time to attend to some small details in the weeks prior to the actual move. Begin by defrosting and eating the food you have kept in the freezer. Whatever is not cooked and eaten will have to be discarded a few days before the move, so use it or lose it. The same goes for the pantry and food storage cabinets. Use the left over pasta and sauces. Spices, and unopened cans and packages can usually relocate with you. I recommend that you do not move items such as vegetable oil since breakage could cause a major mess. If you feel you must bring your almost full bag of sugar, please put it in a tightly closed plastic container or at least surround it with a large zip lock bag. Do not even think about saving any of your food items if you are storing your belongings. Even the cleanest pest treated storage facility may have unwanted critters crawling about. I am sure you won't want to welcome them to your new home. It is best to dispose of almost all of your remaining food since it is all easily replaced. Canned goods are usually cheap and add unnecessary weight to your move. Give any extras to a food bank. We only take items from our spice rack and full adult beverage bottles because they are more costly to replace than most consumables.

Go to your local post office or visit www.usps.com to obtain a change of address kit. Carefully fill out the forms which ask for your current address, your future address and the specific date to begin forwarding your mail to your new location. The packet will probably also contain some change of address cards. Mail is typically only forwarded for a few months so it is important to let others know about your new address as soon as possible. Notify your friends, relatives, business associates and credit card companies about your new residence with a change of address card or email. You can have your magazine subscriptions move with you too by calling OneSwitch at 1–800–508–6307 during business hours. You can also contact each magazine or newspaper individually by phone or email, but OneSwitch will save you some time. Just have your subscription information handy when placing the call.

Next, pull out all your recently received or paid utility statements. Set them in front of you with paper and pen. Call each one to inform them of your upcoming move. Arrange to have all services (gas, electric, water, sewage, telephone, cable and waste removal) disconnected or ceased on a specific date and give each one the new address where they can send final billings. Be sure to have the utilities on through the date of closing and instruct the buyer to establish service in his or her name on the following date. Usually realtors will remind their clients of this duty, but just be sure all are aware of your actions. You are certainly not obligated to pay for any utilities once a new owner has taken possession of your old property. If you are moving from a rental home, you will also need to make all applicable calls informing each utility provider of your moving dates and new address. If you are moving within the same area, you will simply tell the utilities when you want service to end at one address and when to begin at the new one. If you are moving outside the region, you will have to get the contact information for the providers in your new location and phone, email or FAX them with the necessary information so that service can be established in your new home when you arrive. Some of these companies may require deposits and credit checks. I usually set aside an afternoon to make all these calls. This way I have all the information in front of me at one time and get it all done without any confusion.

Notify any other service people you use, such as lawn care providers, home cleaners and pool maintenance providers of your move. Give them final work dates and pay them in full when they finish their job. If you are moving locally and have been satisfied with their performance, simply give them your new address and ask them to follow you to your new place.

Most of us have come to depend upon our cellular phones and find it difficult to live without them. If you are moving outside of your current area code, do not think you need to cancel your cell phone number and get one with the area code of your new location. Most cell phone contracts now allow you to take your phone number anywhere you go and still pay the same charge per minute. Cingular Wireless, for example has a nationwide plan that charges the same fee no matter where you are calling to or calling from. If you change your phone number to your new area code before your current contract has expired, you will probably be charged a high termination fee. Carefully review the terms of your service provider's contract to see how long you are obligated to them before you make even the slightest change. Even a slight alteration in your plan or updating your phone can add to the length of your contract.

If you have a school aged child or children, you need to go to their current school(s) and request copies of each child's records. Let your child's school personnel know when you will be removing your child from their school and when he or she will start at their new school. They may request the address of the new school and ask you to authorize them to send the official transcripts directly there. Sometimes even with your identification and signature, schools are reluctant to make copies of transcripts and records for you to carry. You have the right to see your student's files and review them until the child reaches eighteen years of age. This is a good time to examine the records for accuracy. I imagine each district, state and private school has its own rules about handling these records. Call or make an appointment to go in to the office to learn how the current school wants to handle transferring your child's information to the new school. I also suggest you schedule a meeting with the teacher(s) to review your child's progress and request her or him to write down some recommendations to be shared with the new faculty. When we moved from Pennsylvania, our oldest daughter was in kindergarten. The school and teacher were so helpful. They gave me all of her records and provided detailed information and suggestions for her new teacher. This allowed the new teacher to know exactly what our daughter had accomplished and what she was ready to handle in her new class. She transitioned easily into her new environment with the help of the kind and caring staffs of both schools.

Tell all of your doctors, your dentist, your church or synagogue leaders, and your veterinarian about your upcoming move. Ask if they know of any physicians, dentists, places of worship, or vets in your new location that they can recommend. Request copies of your medical records to have on hand in case of any emergency. Vets will gladly give you copies of Spot's medical file that you can just hand deliver to the new vet. Physicians usually prefer to mail your records after you have found a new doctor in your new location. Since it can take a bit of time to locate new doctors, I insist on having copies of our records. Doing this requires your signature and often a charge for each page copied. I have been able to carry mammogram and dental X rays with me too. I am sure each doctor has his/her own way of transferring patients, so you may want to call each office manager to inquire about the process.

I also suggest you talk with your bank about transferring your accounts to your new location. If you do your banking at large establishments, all your information will be in their computer systems and easily accessible at the branch near your new home. If there is no convenient location, you will probably want to begin closing your bank accounts and establish new ones as soon as you get to your new address. The bank will remind you that all checks must be cleared before you can close a checking account. The bank will probably want all account change requests in writing. The bank will issue you a check for the remaining balance on all your accounts once they are closed. Keep records of these closings to insure you do not get charged monthly service fees for accounts that are no longer open. The bank we patronized while living in New York continued to send us statements showing monthly service debits on accounts that were empty and closed. Luckily we kept our final paperwork and sent the institution copies with a second letter requesting closure. All was finally resolved and the fees were removed from our account.

As for current medications, I recommend you check with your pharmacy about transferring established prescriptions to your new location. The pharmacy can FAX your ongoing prescriptions to your new pharmacy. Large chains such as Walgreens or CVS have sites all over the country that can easily enable you to obtain your medications without any trouble by accessing your information by computer. In the event you cannot find a convenient location or you use a small pharmacy, your prescriptions can still be transferred rather easily. Your new pharmacist will probably just need to speak by phone to your previous pharmacist and handle it electronically. I advise you to ask ahead of time and bring plenty of your required medications with you to keep you healthy in case of any pharmaceutical delays.

This may sound silly to some men, but ladies, another person you will want to inform about your move is your favorite hairstylist and colorist. We often develop a bond with our beauty providers so you will want to explain when you will be leaving. When you visit your hair stylist for the last time, it is a good idea to ask him or her to write down your coloring formula on the back of a business card. A recent photograph of yourself having a "good hair day" can also help the new stylist see how you want to look. Any information you can give the new hairdresser at your first appointment will help him/her continue serving your beauty needs in the manner you already like.

Lastly, make travel arrangements for your family to get from point A to point B. If you are driving a long distance you may need to make hotel reservations for stops along the way. If you are flying you will need to book your flights and arrange for transportation to and from the airport. It is likely you will require a couple of nights in a hotel too. Keep all receipts in your moving file since these are all relocation expenses for later reimbursement or possible tax return deductions. If Fluffy is flying with you, you will need to inform the ticket agent and he will give you specific instructions about pet carriers, veterinary health certificates and applicable fees. I urge you to think and prepare ahead to avoid any glitches along the way. Pay attention to the details.

- Relax and take a brief break.

- Eat or empty the contents of your freezer during the weeks prior to moving.

- Discard or eat the contents of your refrigerator and pantry in the days before moving.

- Donate your non-perishable foods if you are moving a long distance or using storage.

- Fill out change of address forms at the post office or at www.usps.com.

- Notify your friends, relatives and business associates of your new address.

- Notify the magazines and newspapers you subscribe to of your new address.

- Call all service providers to arrange for disconnection dates and final billings.

- Contact all service providers in the new location to establish service.

- Notify hired helpers of final work dates and pay them in full.

- Review your cell phone contract. Wait until it expires to make any service changes.

- Request copies of your child's school records and provide address of new school.

- Ask your child's teacher to give you a progress report to share with the new teacher.

- Request all medical records and recommendations from your dentist, doctors and vet.

- Talk to your bank about transferring all accounts to the new location or closing them.

- Have your pharmacist transfer all prescriptions to the branch in your new area.

- Ask your hair colorist for your formula so you can share it with your new hairdresser.

- Make all necessary travel arrangements to get you and your family to your new home.

13 | Packing Up

By now you have determined whether you are paying professional packers or doing the work yourself. Obviously, hiring packers is the easiest and quickest way to get through this part of the relocation process, but it is not always practical or financially possible. If you have ample time and are moving nearby than you can gradually move your things a few boxes at a time starting with the luxury items and ending with the essentials. When the budget is tight, self packing is usually the best choice. Regardless of the method you select, packing is a crucial step because everything you own is going with you to your new location. You can truly think of this step as "taking everything but the kitchen sink!"

As I have said earlier, professional packers are wonderful, but it is essential that you are prepared for their arrival. Decide how you want to handle your houseplants. Are you taking them with you in your vehicle or are you leaving them behind with neighbors? Movers will usually only take silk versions. You must have the items you are bringing yourself such as your jewelry, toiletries, important files and suitcases set aside and specially marked or they will pack these too. I even had a mover that packed my trash cans with trash in them. You can bet that was not a nice surprise on the other end! Better yet, put these things in your locked car before the workers even get to your front door to avoid any confusion. Clearly mark the objects such as appliances which are not going on the truck with red tags or something else very visible. I have learned to place items such as extra keys, garage remote controls, appliance warranties and owner's manuals, and phone books in one drawer labeled "do not pack." I made the mistake once of not separating these things and had to pay shipping to have them sent back to the couple that bought our home. Everything that is supposed to stay with the home needs to remain there.

If possible, try to have a friend or two at your house with you so there are extra eyes keeping watch on how things are being done. The packers usually work so quickly that is hard to keep tabs on everything, everywhere by yourself. We have had some items mysteriously vanish somewhere along the way. I am not necessarily accusing anyone of anything, but since we never found our hand held television or a few small family heirlooms, I suspect some foul play. Without any proof, such as an eye witness, there was nothing I could do. Since there is much confusion at this time, I advise you to continually walk around or station friends in specific areas to watch as items are going into boxes.

Carry around permanent marking pens and add more detailed contents descriptions to the boxes than the packers do. It is probably not good to write something like "gold coin collection" on the outside since it might attract a thief, but a few details will simplify unpacking. Typically the packers will only mark the box with the name of the room it came from and that's it. Some of them will be more specific if you ask them to be, but you will probably want to label the boxes yourself with more information since it will be helpful to know where some of your favorite or essential belongings are located. We found it very annoying when we could not find the sheets to our bed, the remote controls for the televisions or the alarm clock for several days. We eventually found them in a box marked "computer" and another marked "games." Once, I even filed a claim with the moving company when I could not find our silver service. Imagine how shocked I was when I discovered all twelve place settings packed in a box labeled *Christmas Decorations!* Avoid the same frustration by adding your own notes to each carton.

Also, it is imperative that you get complete copies of the inventory list from the movers before they leave. Every single box, crate and piece of furniture should be itemized, described, numbered and inspected for condition at point of origination. The driver will go over the paperwork with you and ask you to initial and/or sign each page indicating everything belonging to you that has been loaded on the truck. This serves as proof of everything you entrusted to their care. Keep these papers handy along with contact phone numbers as you travel to your new home. You will need them when the truck is being unloaded. At your destination the inventory list will also serve as a check list to assure you that all your belongings have arrived. Hang on to these forms since you may also need to refer to them in the event you find it necessary to file a claim against the mover for lost or damaged goods. Also, just before the truck pulls away, confirm the delivery date and time so you know specifically when to expect to see the driver and your valuables at your new address.

Self packers should begin rolling up their sleeves at least a couple weeks before the move out date. Begin by deciding where you are going to get your cartons. You can purchase them from a moving company, an office supply store, a home improvement store, a shipping company or a do-it-yourself moving company.

I have found cartons and packing supplies to be less expensive at the do-it-yourself type places. They have many types and sizes of boxes and all the tape and protective wrapping paper and supplies you need at reasonable prices. You can save some money by asking your grocery store if you can have some of the boxes from their next delivery. They might be willing to help you instead of quickly crushing them as soon as they are empty. It's worth asking. Liquor stores are another good source since they have sturdy boxes which are great for packing glassware and small breakables. Stop in there and ask if they would save some boxes for you too.

Start packing the items you can function without first. Knick knacks, wall décor and out of season clothing all fall into this category. Always put the heavier items in the bottom of the container and the lighter things on top. Never overload a box by making it too heavy because it could fall apart or injure someone. Securely tape the bottom and top of each box in two directions with tape meant for this purpose. Invest in strong packing tape and a sturdy tape dispenser. If the bottom falls out of a box, you have a potential disaster. Clearly mark every box with its contents and indicate which room you want it placed in when it arrives at your new home. As I mentioned before, taking the time to do this will make things much easier when you are moving in.

Buy paper plates, paper napkins, plastic cups and plastic utensils about a week before moving out. These and the minimal contents of your refrigerator will soon become the only supplies left in your kitchen. Get going on the kitchen since you probably have lots to pack from this room and you will be too busy to cook or grocery shop for anything anyway. Allocate plenty of cartons for the kitchen since you are likely to have more tucked away in the cabinets than you think. Allow ample time to pack it all too. Ordering out, dining out, carrying out and then throwing away the dishes is the easiest way to handle things at this point. You must disconnect and open the doors on the refrigerator several days before the move if you plan to take it with you. Defrosting ahead of time allows it to dry out properly and prevents water damage to your other belongings.

Some packing tips to assure minimal or no breakage include: place a pillow, towels or crumpled paper at the bottom of all boxes that will contain breakables; individually wrap all drinking glasses, vases, glass plates and other breakables in wrapping paper or bubble wrap; always stand glassware and vases up instead of laying them on their sides. All plates, trays, frames containing glass, mirrors and glass table tops should also be placed on end and not flat. Wrap televisions, large wall décor and computers with blankets, bedspreads or oversized beach towels. Slide large flat breakables between two mattresses for extra protection. Use old blankets to cover furniture and secure drawers with soft rope so they do not come loose during transport. Insert extra paper or padding along the sides and top of all boxes containing fragile items. Load and pack a truck as tightly as possible so that shifting of contents is less likely. Always put heavier boxes on the bottom and then stack lighter boxes on top. Use a loading ramp and dolly to help prevent injury to yourself and your helpers. You may want to buy thick rope and cords to help secure your belongings inside the truck as well.

Once all appears to be loaded on the rental truck or mover's van, take a second and third walk around your house to be sure everything that is supposed to make the trip is gone. Thoroughly check every drawer, closet, cabinet and shelf for any stray items. Keep in mind that anything left behind is likely to become the property of whoever moves in.

I strongly suggest you take the time to clean the place before you leave for the last time. Borrow the vacuum of a neighbor or ask the movers to load it last. Run it over all the floors and use the attachment to quickly clean cabinet shelves and drawers. Use a glass or all purpose cleaner and paper towels to spruce up the bathrooms and kitchen counters. If you sold the house, the buyers are probably going to do a "final walk through" in which the realtors meet them at the property once again to inspect for damages that may have occurred since they contracted to purchase the home. They will also want to make sure that anything they may have included in that contract is not missing. I am certain they will appreciate having the home in good condition.

Rental property should also be cleaned since the landlord will probably charge a cleaning fee if you leave anything dirty. I have always taken the extra time to leave every place I have ever lived spotless. Every buyer has commented on the kindness of my efforts, and we have always gotten our full security deposit back from every rental property. If your schedule is too tight or you simply do not want to clean, hire someone to do it for you.

- Decide whether to take house plants with you or leave them with friends.

- Separate and clearly mark items you plan to carry with you.

- Place items such as appliance manuals in a drawer marked "do not pack."

- Mark items you are not moving with "do not move" stickers.

- Ask a couple friends to help you keep tabs on the packers' progress.

- Add detailed descriptions to cartons as they are packed to ease item location later.

- Get the complete inventory list before movers leave. Keep this for the moving in day.

- Self packers need to locate packing materials at least two weeks before moving.

- Begin packing items you can live without such as decorative items and knick knacks.

- Purchase disposable plates, cups and utensils one week prior to moving.

- Pack up the kitchen contents. You won't have time to cook anyway.

- Pull the plug on the refrigerator and open its doors a few days before transporting.

- Pack up the rest of your belongings using the tips included in chapter thirteen.

- Walk around checking cabinets, drawers and closets for anything left behind.

- Clean the place before you leave for the final time. This is a nice thing to do.

14 | Property Settlements

Whether you are transferring ownership of your current home to a buyer or you are purchasing a property, you will have to complete the transaction at what is called the closing or the settlement. As I mentioned in chapter ten, settlement practices often vary from location to location. In some of the western states, closings are handled by escrow agents. Both parties provide appropriate funds and documents and there is no formal meeting. In some areas settlements are performed by attorneys, real estate brokers, lenders, title insurance companies or escrow companies. Learn in advance how these transactions take place where you are so that you are thoroughly prepared and can hire the appropriate professional if necessary.

Work with all professionals involved to make sure that everything is in order to proceed with the closing. Your real estate agent should confirm that all contingencies in the sales agreement have been satisfied. Are all loans approved and has the property passed all inspections following any requested repairs? If your state requires a termite clearance letter, insist that this is available at least a week before you pass papers in the event that treatment and another inspection is needed. The lending agent must lock in or confirm your interest rate well in advance so you know exactly what your payments will be. The appropriate professional, usually the closing attorney, will inform you in advance of any unusual problems associated with the title search and property survey that may cause a delay or cancellation of sale. Submit proof of homeowners insurance and title insurance to the closing attorney well before the closing in case the lender finds anything unsatisfactory requiring changes.

A final walk-through of the property will be scheduled a few days before the settlement date. Usually the real estate agent meets the buyer at the property and they slowly and carefully tour the house and the grounds looking for any problems that may require attention. The formal inspection report is usually used as a reference to ensure that all concerns have been corrected. The home should be empty and in the condition specified in the contract. If any troubles are detected, they should be put in writing as addendums to the contract so the seller is aware of all the obligations needed to be fulfilled before the property can change hands. New construction also requires a final inspection. Insist that the builder completes all work on the house before closing. Minor cosmetic work is often allowable and can be addressed through a "punch list" of items needing to be fixed after closing. It is best to withhold some funds from the builder to keep them motivated to complete all unfinished work and repairs. Some builders seem to disappear as soon as they have all their money. We held back several thousand dollars from a builder until he completed a few unfinished projects specified in our sales agreement. Believe me, he wanted his money and got the jobs done very quickly! Most reputable construction companies provide at least a one year warranty which allows ample time for you to discover trouble spots and to schedule repairs. Warranties and guarantees should be documented and well understood by both parties before closing.

Sometimes it becomes necessary for a member of one of the parties to be absent from the actual closing. This happened when family obligations prevented me from attending a settlement. We simply contacted our attorney and he compiled the necessary forms enabling me to give my husband "power of attorney" or the authority to act on my behalf. Today's technology has made all of this so much easier when we can FAX signed documents back and forth in just minutes. If a conflict arises, contact your lawyer as soon as possible so that the applicable paperwork can be drawn up and signed, allowing your closing to proceed as scheduled.

Your closing professional is required to provide a complete settlement statement to you at least one full day prior to the scheduled closing. Compare the numbers from the earlier "good faith estimate" I mentioned in chapter eight that you received at the time you applied for your mortgage. Specific settlement costs will be itemized on this statement. Contract sales price, broker's commission, numerous fees associated with obtaining the loan, escrow deposits, title charges, insurance costs, taxes, attorney fees, recording and transfer charges, survey costs, inspection charges and any other applicable expenses must be detailed in the settlement statement. Take adequate time to carefully examine these documents. If you discover any variations, you should ask for full explanations. Determine how the closing costs are to be paid and to whom they are to be paid. You will probably have to have certified or cashier's checks prepared to bring with you to closing. Find out if you need to bring any additional documents to closing such as specific forms of identification or further evidence to satisfy funding requirements specified in your loan approval letter. Any and all concerns and details must be addressed and attended to before the actual time of settlement to avoid possible delays and unpleasant surprises. Do not hesitate to ask any questions. Remember you are making a very large investment and the associated professionals are working for you. You have the right, as the buyer or the seller, to feel as comfortable, informed and as prepared as possible when you close on a property.

Lastly, double check exactly where and when the closing will take place. Again, states and counties determine how real estate transactions are performed. Most often our property closings have been held at law firms. Some have been at real estate offices, others at escrow agencies and even government buildings. Once we had to appear at a county court house in New York where we were escorted into a huge room full of people sitting around tables all signing similar documents for other settlements. There was no privacy and it seemed like a production line. I realize that property transfers are matters of public record, but that seemed a bit too impersonal to me. Know ahead of time where you are to report and come well prepared.

I hope I have not made this all sound too complex. Remember that people just like you and me are buying and selling real estate everyday and these transactions usually go quite smoothly. Hiccups are almost always very small and quickly remedied. Everyone involved wants to see the transaction take place. I have never had a closing delayed at the last minute or not take place. Bring your reading glasses and a fresh pen to closing because you will autograph what seems like a mountain of paperwork. Take your time and feel free to ask questions about what you are signing so you fully understand the details. You have come a long way to get to this day. Congratulations on closing the deal!

- Learn in advance how property transfers are handled in your new area.

- Hire the appropriate professionals to represent and help you with the transaction.

- Get your realtor to confirm that all contract contingencies have been satisfied.

- Confirm that all loans and interest rates are locked in so exact payments are known.

- Make sure that the title search and property survey are satisfactorily completed.

- Obtain proof of homeowner's and title insurance.

- Schedule a final walk through of the empty property a few days before closing.

- Inspect the property during the walk through. Use the inspector's report as a guide.

- Notify the seller of any problems needing improvement prior to closing.

- Walk through new construction too. Note incomplete work and repairs at closing.

- Withhold money at closing for new construction until all work is done correctly.

- Prepare the "punch list(s)" for the builder to be handled during the warranty period.

- Obtain "power of attorney" if either you or your spouse is unable to attend the closing.

- Obtain the complete settlement statement at least one full business day prior to closing.

- Compare the estimate figures to the statement. Discuss and resolve any variances.

- Find out exactly what you need to bring to closing. Gather all required paperwork.

- Check on the time and place of the closing. Arrive promptly and prepared.

- Bring reading glasses and pens. Read everything and ask questions before signing.

- Treat yourself to a special lunch or dinner to celebrate your new home!

15 | Moving In

The time has finally arrived! You are ready to move into your new home! Hopefully the movers are nearby and they have given you the information you need to pay them accurately, when and only when, the job is completed. Call the company's contact number if you haven't received these details at least a day before delivery. Know exactly what type of payment they accept and the amount. The actual amount may even be a little lower than you were quoted because the load may have weighed less than the original estimate. The amount should never exceed the quoted estimate. Remember your shipping charges are based mostly on weight and distance. Twice my husband and I were delighted to end up with a lower bill than we had expected. If the movers prefer a check, a money order or cashier's check, find out who it is to be made out to and take care of this business the day before moving in. Avoid any misunderstandings by preparing payment in advance.

Start your move-in day by running into the store to pick up some simple snacks and beverages since you will need to refuel yourself and your helpers during the busy day ahead. Then take a walk around your new place and try to visualize where you want your furnishings placed. The unloading process will be easier for all involved if you can quickly indicate where you want things to go. For example, show your helpers and movers where you want the beds, the dressers, the sofa and the televisions so they know right where to take them before they even begin to take things off the truck.

I urge you to find a couple friends to stay with you during the inevitable chaos. This is especially important if you have professional movers deliver your goods. Station a reliable helper right at the front door. This person will have the important job of checking off each numbered item on the inventory list as it is brought into your home. The movers sometimes call these numbers off rapidly so whoever does this job must be alert and able to stay on task throughout the entire unloading process. I have found it nearly impossible to simultaneously handle this clerical role while walking around directing the workers to placement spots. If you are fortunate enough to have another helper, ask him or her to examine the condition of your things and keep notes of any boxes or furniture that looks damaged while you continue supervising the movers. You can then precisely point out any problems to the movers and make notes on the paperwork before they pull away. Unfortunately, I was alone twice during the move-in process. Both times, some things were unaccounted for and other items were misplaced or poorly treated since I could not be in three or more places at once. If you have yet to develop friendships in a new area or have no family nearby, I recommend you still make arrangements to have someone you trust with you on moving in day. It is simply too difficult to do efficiently on your own.

Sometimes people pay a moving service to unpack their things too. I have only done this once and found it extremely overwhelming. The workers all wanted to know at the same time where to put everything and I really was not sure where I wanted the knick knacks or which drawer was best suited to store kitchen utensils. Our belongings were strewn everywhere and the mountains of packing paper seemed insurmountable. After a couple of hours, I sent them on their way. Friends have told me this is the ideal method of moving in, but it is not for me. It is probably wonderful to rapidly rid your house of all the boxes and paper, but I prefer to take my time, unpack gradually and decide where to place things as I become more comfortable with my new surroundings. If you are able to make placement decisions extremely quickly, you may want to try hiring the unpacking squad. Decide what you think will work best for you.

When it appears that all has been unloaded and the movers have done the job they have been hired to do, it is time to carefully compare your inventory list with the mover's list. Be certain that all items have been accounted for and note anything that appears damaged. If something seems to be missing, look everywhere in and around the house as well as in the truck. Chances are the thing(s) will be found. Further protect yourself in the event you later discover other damage or breakage by writing your own addendum on the forms stating that unpacked cartons cannot be examined until all unpacking is completed. Initial next to this sentence and have the driver initial it too. If you do not add this to the paperwork, your signature may mean that you accept your shipment in its current condition. As always, read everything carefully and thoroughly before signing. Finally, hand the driver the prepared means of payment. Tip the crew if they have done the job to your satisfaction. I generally give them enough for a nice hearty meal. After a hard day's work, they will appreciate this kindness.

Now, be kind to yourself. Take a break, put your feet up and then go out to eat. If you plan to stay in your new place the first night, locate your bedding and then collapse for a much deserved restful sleep. Sweet dreams!

- Check on the form of payment and amount with the movers the day before delivery.

- Prepare the mover's payment as requested.

- Purchase and bring snacks and beverages to the new house.

- Walk around and visualize placement of your furnishings before the movers arrive.

- Ask a couple of reliable friends to help you move into your new home.

- Prepare yourself to make snap placement decisions if you hired movers to unpack.

- Compare your inventory list with the mover's list when all appears to be unloaded.

- Note anything that seems to be missing or obviously damaged from the inventory lists.

- Add an addendum stating you will notify them of any damages once all is unpacked.

- Insist that the driver initial the addendum.

- Pay the mover only when all is unloaded, inventory is checked and concerns noted.

- Tip the moving crew if they have done a good job. Treat yourself and your helpers to a hearty casual dinner.

- Relax and have a restful night's sleep. Tomorrow will be a busy day.

16 | Getting Settled

Yea, you are now in your new home! Pat yourself on the back for all that you have accomplished. You are nearing the end of your moving journey, but do not stop now. If you have had professionals unpack for you, you may feel somewhat organized, if not, you have quite a bit of work to do. If you had the moving company pack for you, examine your goods throughout the unpacking process for any damages and note container and item numbers for making claims later. I have always started the unpacking ordeal with the bedrooms because I know I will want to sleep in my own bed as soon as possible. I look for the linens first and make up the beds. Somehow everyplace begins to look like home when the beds are made. Next, I put away clothing and toiletries. Focus on organizing the bedrooms and baths first since you will need to utilize these rooms almost immediately. Everyone wants to rest comfortably and have the ability to fully use the bathrooms. Keep in mind that you can still go out to eat or do without the electronics for another day or two.

After you have completed the bedrooms and bathrooms, move into the kitchen. You are probably anxious to find your coffee pot and dishes. Going out, eating fast food and carry out are probably getting old by now. You will be glad to be able to cook and eat in your own home. Take your time with this area because there are lots of breakables which require careful unwrapping. Try to place items in appropriate places where they are easily accessible for their intended use. For example, pots and pans should be near the stove, plates and cups are usually near the dishwasher, and dishtowels and dish soap are often by the sink. Do not hurry with this important room. You are likely to make adjustments as you find places for all your kitchen items.

By now, you have acquired many empty boxes and an enormous amount of packing paper. I have always filled my garage with this stuff and assigned my husband with the job of breaking down the cartons and filling garbage bags with paper. Of course, he does not enjoy this task, but he is always thrilled when the garage is empty enough to park his car inside. If you do not have a helpful husband or a garage to throw the waste into, you will need to use a reliable box cutter to remove the clutter as you empty each container. Purchase plenty of large strong garbage bags to handle all the paper. If you have a trash compactor, use it to crush the packing material so you can get as much into each trash bag as possible. Find out when the garbage collectors come by and put out as much as they allow. Call to ask if you can arrange for a large pickup once you have finished unpacking all your cartons. There may be an extra charge for this service, but it is well worth it. If you are in an apartment or condominium complex, you can probably place all moving boxes and packing paper in a large dumpster near your unit.

As soon as I have finished the kitchen, I unpack the living areas. My husband sets up the television, stereo and other electronics. I schedule the cable installation before moving in so that the electronics all work as soon as possible. Most men find it difficult to exist too long without live sporting event broadcasts. While he enjoys his electronic entertainment, I arrange the bookshelves and unpack lamps and other accessories. For the time being, I stand all wall art against an empty wall to get it out of the way. I will determine where it will go later. Some of it will work nicely in the new place, some may not. Sometimes the picture you had hanging over your bed looks better in the family room over the sofa. The art you enjoyed in your foyer may now enhance your dining room instead. You may not even find a suitable spot for a favorite piece. If this occurs, save it since you are likely to move again someday, give it to a friend who has admired it, or donate it to a worthy charity. You will need to be a bit flexible and creative as you strive to find homes for all your things.

I complete the unpacking in the garage and then the basement. Hopefully you have little to store in either place since you should have gotten rid of all unused and unneeded belongings prior to moving. Your household tools, sports equipment and gardening supplies should be located in the garage. If you don't already have them, buy shelving or cabinetry to store all these things. Holiday decorations and other important but infrequently utilized items should be placed in a storage closet or tucked away in the basement or garage.

You are finally moved in and the boxes are gone!! Relax and watch a good movie on the recently connected DVD player. You are almost at the finish line. There are only a few more details to deal with and you will be settled.

Chapter Sixteen Check List

- Leave the stickers on your furniture and boxes until you examine for damage and loss.

- Find your linens, make up your beds and unpack your bedrooms.

- Note any damage you discover as you unpack. Use sticker numbers to identify items.

- Put away clothing.

- Unpack and organize the bathrooms.

- Unpack and organize your kitchen.

- Place the packing paper in large, strong garbage bags. Break down the boxes.

- Put packing waste out for trash collection or call waste company for a large pick up.

- Unpack and set up the living areas and electronics.

- Unpack the garage.

- Unpack the basement.

- Store infrequently used items in the attic, storage closet or basement.

- Hang artwork and place accessories.

- Donate, store or give away items you find unsuitable for this house.

- Relax, you are almost done.

17 | Home Sweet Home

You have just about completed your relocation ordeal. Most people feel that moving is one of life's most difficult and stressful tasks, so you should be proud of yourself for making it thus far; but you are not quite finished. Your house should now be in order with boxes unpacked, utilities working and all rooms functional. You only have a few organizational duties to perform in order to make your new place a home. You still need to familiarize yourself with your new surroundings, find new service and health care providers, fulfill some legal obligations, file claims if necessary with your movers, and get to know your neighbors.

Since all your boxes are now empty and the contents should have been examined, it is time to decide if you need to file a damage report and claim with your moving company. Remember from chapter fifteen you noted on the final bill of lading that you reserved the right to still make claims on the condition of your goods and the contents of cartons which remained unopened when the driver left your property. Follow through with this right away if you discover any damages within cartons which they packed or furniture damage you had no opportunity to closely observe during the hectic delivery day. Call the moving company to request the necessary forms to facilitate your claim. Fill out the forms with as much detail as possible and attach the inventory list along with a cover letter asking for a quick response to your requests for repairs or replacement values. As always, keep copies of everything until all is settled to your satisfaction. If you have paid for full value coverage as I encouraged you to do in chapter eleven, you should have little or no trouble having your claims resolved. The mover may want to send out an inspector to review your claim, or they may just go ahead and send out a repair person to handle the small dents and nicks. The mover should send you a check to replace items that are broken beyond repair. If you have any trouble dealing with the claims department, contact the corporate office and insist on speaking with an individual in management. Complaint letters to these individuals can be powerful tools to help settle your claim too. Most of my damage has been minimal and I have only had to voice my dissatisfaction and get pushy with one moving company. Hopefully, all goes smoothly for you and your claim is settled rapidly.

Keep an eye on the incoming mail. The post office will only forward mail from your old address for a few months. Update the addresses on any forwarded mail that you still want and need to receive. It is a good idea to print up attractive change of address notes to send to all your friends and relatives. Naturally, you want each of them to have all your new contact information. Including this information in your holiday cards will also help keep your dear ones up to date on your whereabouts. I try to get my holiday cards out very early after a move so that friends and relatives have my new address. Sending an email containing your new address and phone number to everyone on your email buddy list is also a good idea.

When you are brand new to an area, you have lots to learn. Where is the post office, the best shopping center and the library? Sometimes you can get referrals to help you establish yourself in your new area from people you already know. Maybe your doctor or dentist knows of a good healthcare provider in your new location that he or she can recommend. Maybe you have a friend who lives or has lived nearby that can suggest a veterinarian, hair salon, dry cleaner or super market. The realtor you hired to help you find your new home can also be a valuable resource. Of course, he or she should know the area very well and should be able to provide you with a detailed map to help you find your way around as well as give you a list of preferred businesses. If this information is not offered, be sure to ask for it. The previous owner of your house may have done what I have always done, and left you a list of contacts for various services. It is often easiest to continue with the same house cleaning service and yard maintenance people since they are already familiar with the property. If you are displeased after a few weeks, you can look for someone new.

Your neighbors are probably your best source of detailed information about your area. If no one has come by to introduce themselves during the move in days, put a smile on your face and go ring doorbells. All people are busy these days, so don't assume they are not interested in getting to know you. Hopefully, they will be eager to visit with you and share their experiences about your new neighborhood. If your first attempt seems unsuccessful, keep trying. Neighbors can quickly become good friends. We have been fortunate to find neighbors who became close friends everywhere we have lived. Many have remained life-long friends. Neighbors are usually happy to give you the neighborhood "scoop" and to tell you which doctors and dentists to visit, and which window washer, dog sitter, painter etc. to hire. They are also wonderful about watching your house and bringing in your mail when you are away. Reciprocal babysitting can even become the routine when you and your neighbors have children. Get out and meet your neighbors as soon as you can.

Your realtor should be able to provide you with a list of local government offices and phone numbers which you may be required to visit in order to establish full legal residency in your new area. Call your agent to request this information or look on-line for information about your county and state. Most states require you to change your address on your driver's license within a month or two of occupying your new home. If you have moved to a new state, you must register your vehicle(s) and apply for a completely new driver's license. Call in advance or check your state's Department of Motor Vehicle (DMV) website to learn all the details about these requirements and the paperwork you need to bring with you to complete these tasks. Leased vehicles usually cannot be registered in a new state without written permission from the leasing company. Do not be surprised if they ask you to bring multiple forms of identification including a valid driver's license and/or a birth certificate. You will probably need to present an approved proof of residency such as a recent utility bill, bank statement or a mortgage payment coupon. Other required forms may include a completed affidavit naming your vehicle leasing agent or lien holder, a completed title application and a certification of inspection. Proof that your vehicle passed an emissions test is often necessary too. In addition, you will need to bring sufficient funds to pay all the applicable fees. These fees and requirements can very greatly from state to state and even from county to county.

Some states insist that you retake the entire driver's exam. Others ask you to pass an eye test, pay a fee and surrender your old license. In New York and Georgia you can also register to vote at motor vehicle offices. Whatever you do, go prepared and plan to spend a few hours to an entire day fulfilling these government mandates. Waiting for your turn is always so boring, but make it as pleasant as possible by bringing a good book. If possible, do not bring any children with you! It is hard enough for you to endure long lines.

It is always a good idea to purchase a detailed local map if your realtor has not given you one. Your neighborhood supermarket or bookstore should sell them. Pinpoint the location of your home and learn the names of surrounding streets and landmarks. If your car has a navigation system in it, you are lucky. Finding your way around will be simple. Either way, it is helpful to get in your vehicle, drive around and learn the location of the nearest hospital, post office and gas station. If you get temporarily lost, note the closest intersection, drive into a parking lot and refer to your map. You will figure it all out after a few outings. I have had to do this many times and have always been able to get around my new towns after a few trial runs. I have always been directionally challenged, so if I can do it, you certainly can too.

I also suggest you subscribe to the local newspaper. Most papers contain information on the local happenings and concerns to help you learn more about your area. Community calendars are often printed within its pages. This listing of organizations and events can help you meet people with common interests. Attend a local meeting, volunteer for a charity group, attend worship services and visit local attractions. You will be amazed at how quickly you can find interesting people and things to do in your new hometown.

Lastly, you will want to add all the special touches that transform a house into a home. You want your house to reflect your personality and be a refuge for you and your family. Consider a fresh coat of paint, house plants, and additional or alternative decorative touches such as new window treatments, wall art, area rugs, carpeting, and throw pillows. Check out decorating magazines to inspire your creative side. You can do all this within a budget if you make the effort to shop around. You can discover many ideas and find great values at many discount shopping sights. Have fun turning your house into your own haven.

Before I close, I want to congratulate you! I hope this book has helped you along your path of transition. I encourage you to invite family and friends into your new place. Loved ones truly warm a house and make it a home. May you experience many happy times and create many beautiful memories in your new surroundings. Best wishes!

- File a claim with your moving company if you discover anything damaged or missing.

- Keep your inventory list and claim form copies until all is resolved and repaired.

- Update the address for all forwarded mail that you want to continue receiving.

- Notify your friends and relatives of your new contact information.

- Familiarize yourself with your new surroundings by locating post office, bank, etc.

- Introduce yourself to your neighbors. They can make the transition much easier.

- Learn the requirements involved with establishing residency in your new area.

- Gather all necessary documents and fulfill the government mandates in your area.

- Use a detailed local map to learn the surrounding streets and landmarks.

- Buy a local newspaper to learn about the events and concerns of the community.

- Get to know your new hometown by joining interest groups, volunteering, etc.

- Add your own special touches to your house to make it your home.

- Host a housewarming party to bring additional joy into your new home.

- Congratulate yourself on all you have accomplished! Enjoy your new location!

Sources

1. Adams, John. "Inside Advice" The Atlanta Journal-Constitution 10 Jul 2005: Classifieds 6.

2. Adams, John. "Inside Advice" The Atlanta Journal-Constitution 26 Jun 2005: Classifieds 6.

3. Adams, John. "Inside Advice" The Atlanta Journal-Constitution 13 Jun 2005: Classifieds 6.

4. Adams, John. "Inside Advice" The Atlanta Journal-Constitution 18 Jul 2004: Classifieds 6.

5. "Around Town: Tips for selling your own home" The Atlanta Journal-Constitution 29 April 2005: G3.

6. Bank of America Pamphlet: Your Guide to Closing. April 2001

7. Cauley, H.M. "Move it (Don't lose it)" The Atlanta Journal-Constitution 16 Jul 2005 EE1+.

8. Glink, Ilyce "Real Estate Matters: Check out neighborhood before you buy" South Florida Sun-Sentinel Homespot 4

9. Howard, Clark. "Ask Clark Howard" The Atlanta Journal-Constitution 11 Jun 2005: EE7.

10. Hohman, Betsy, Vice President Mortgage Origination, North Shore Community Bank 720 Twelfth Street, Wilmette, IL 60091

11. Murphy, Kevin "Definitions help explain words used in new home hunt" South Florida Sun-Sentinel 3 Jan 2004: Real Estate 1+

12. Paul, Peralte C. "Credit reports free and easy–and online" The Atlanta Journal-Constitution A1+.

13. ReMax Partners Pamphlet. Special Buy/Seller Disclosure. Ft. Lauderdale Jan 2002

14. U.S. Department of Housing and Urban Development. Buying Your Home: Settlement Costs and Helpful Information. Washington. June 1997

15. Yadegar, Jacob "Money Matters: Home Buying Basics" West Side Today Feb 2004 Business 18.

16. Yip, Pamela "Avoiding a costly move" The Atlanta Journal-Constitution 9 Jan 2005: Q8.